THE POLITICAL–MASS MEDIA–RACIAL COMPLEX IN GUYANA

Edited by
Prem Misir

University Press of America,® Inc.
Lanham · Boulder · New York · Toronto · Plymouth, UK

Copyright © 2008 by
University Press of America,® Inc.
4501 Forbes Boulevard
Suite 200
Lanham, Maryland 20706
UPA Acquisitions Department (301) 459-3366

Estover Road
Plymouth PL6 7PY
United Kingdom

Library of Congress Control Number: 2007933447
ISBN-13: 978-0-7618-3873-9 (paperback : alk. paper)
ISBN-10: 0-7618-3873-2 (paperback : alk. paper)

Table of Contents

MEDIA

RACE

List of Tables

Politics

Race

Foreword

This invigorating work by Dr. Prem Misir is worth reading by both the social scientists as well as the general public. This volume comprises of papers, essays and commentaries presented by Dr. Misir over a period of time on the political and social development in contemporary Guyana. It has been sectionalized in three areas: Politics & Economic Development, the Mass Media, and, Race & Ethnic Relations.

The author in these essays forcefully brings home the point to us how the concepts of freedom, good order and equality can be differently interpreted by politicians and their parties to suit their circumstances at a particular moment, much to their advantage.

In crystal clear terms, Dr. Misir informs us of the challenges facing this new and fledgling democracy. He bunked critics who argued that the results of the elections for 1997 and 2001 were not reflective of the will of the Guyanese electorate. In a very lucid manner, he drew comparisons of leadership styles in the pre and post 1992 and argued that with the restoration of democracy, the consultative process has been strengthened. He articulated that the charges of victimization, discrimination and marginalization could not be sustained since they were made merely to fuel public discord, division and resentment a charged atmosphere in Guyana.

He then analyses the role of the mass media and highlighted the many challenges facing the nation by virtue of professional journalism. In this regard, the reader is left with the clear position that a proper media code in an urgent imperative.

Dr. Misir's scholarship and prolific research and the issues of race and ethnic relations were brought to bear on analyses which he has conducted on our own problems of divisiveness. He has obviously enlightened us to a path where Guyanese, irrespective of their race, class, or political thinking can live and work together for the enhancement of a true Guyanese nation grounded in pluralist unity.

This work is appealing and will touch the sentiments of all Guyanese who yearn for a better Guyana. That it will enjoy wide circulation is my fervent hope.

Dr. Nanda Kissore Gopaul
Permanent Secretary, Office of the President
Government of Guyana
September 14, 2006

Preface

The new millennium is now here, with the new youthful generation of today interacting with previous generations who were witnesses to the genesis of the political turmoil in Guyana. Essentially, the nature of this political conflict is similar to previous years, except that today, it presents itself with greater intensity and frequency. Incredibly, amid all this mayhem, the country as a whole plods along, silently dismissing the purveyors of this political hostility.

Since 1992, the year in which democracy returned to Guyana after being on the absentee list for some 28 years, some sections of the society have shown considerable reluctance to accept electoral defeat. This disinclination to concede electoral loss graciously is all the more amazing, as the three national election results since 1992 were validated as free, fair, and transparent by reputable international observers.

An important issue on which to focus is what these people are anyway who blatantly and continuously refuse to accept and engage in reason and rationality. These people are part of a community of irrationality, a group of persons with similar social origins and social network. Today, they are institutionalized in an anti 'democracy' political/mass media/racial complex.

When C. Wright Mills alluded to the political/military/industrial complex in the United States, he was attempting to determine who rules America. In the case of Guyana, knowledge of the workings of the political/mass media/racial complex may give some indication as to 'who' and 'what' are responsible for acts inimical to nation building. Since the return to democracy in 1992, destabilization efforts have been in vogue, and this triad complex may very well be a significant factor in the 'destabilization' equation.

One popular political destabilization effort is the now all too familiar post-elections violence that has graduated to becoming a characteristic feature of social life. The outcomes of this senseless violence have really battered the economy. Further, in the absence of a broadcast law in the mass media, there is anarchy, especially on the television. Media reports lacking in accuracy, balance, and fundamental fairness, and laced with racial hatred, are definitively the functions of destabilization. So too is the use of the ethnic/race card, particularly potent at or near elections, to subvert nation building. Clearly, the current ethnic conflict is a weapon invariably used as a subterfuge, enabling political aspirants to gain advantage at electoral times. At the conclusion of an election and its aftermath, this ethnic conflict regresses into protracted hibernation.

In general, the political/mass media/racial complex perseveres in destabilizing the society, making nation building quite problematic, despite some level of sustained progress in the society. This complex essentially is a community of irrationality, engaged in a persisting dissemination of despair.

The papers are classified into three sections: Politics and Economic Development; Mass Media; and Race and Ethnic Relations. In fact, the articles relate partly to the political/mass media/racial complex that is inhabited by a community of irrationality. The Guyana Chronicle carried these articles between 2001 through 2006; two objectives could be discussed: one, to demonstrate the modus operandi and dysfunctional consequences of this community of irrationality, through the political/mass media/racial complex, in the process of nation building; and two, to show the rational behaviors that hold the society together through the progress made since 1992. It is hoped that those who are able to see this community of irrationality as the producer of destabilization, will create for themselves the next chapter in totally neutralizing this political/mass media/racial complex.

Ms. Sophia Collier, Personal Assistant, Office of the Pro-Chancellor, University of Guyana, gave invaluable assistance in preparing and formatting the book for publication; she, indeed, was a great asset, ensuring compliance with rigid timelines.

Prem Misir
September 13, 2006

Politics

The December 7, 1964 Elections: A Betrayal of Trust

Guyana became a pronounced item on the foreign policy agenda for both the U.S. and British Governments in the 1950s and 1960s. The U.S. and British Governments had concerns over the People's Progressive Party (PPP) Administration's perceived close ties to Moscow and Cuba. The early 1950s in the U.S. witnessed the McCarthy witch-hunt against communism, and the beginnings of the Cold War with a rhetorically running battle between the U.S. and the former Soviet Union.

December 7

Last Tuesday December 7 marked forty years for the infamous 1964 Election Day in British Guiana (now Guyana). The U.S. and British Governments imposed this election upon the people in a bid to remove the PPP from office through a new electoral arrangement called Proportional Representation (PR). The results of this election were:

Table 1.1: Election Results from 1964

Party	Votes, 1964	% Votes, 1961	% Votes, 1964
PPP	109,332	42.6	45.8
PNC	96,567	40.9	40.5
UF	26,612	16.3	12.4
GUMP	1,194	---	---
JP	1,334	---	---
PEP	224	---	---
NLF	177	---	---

The PPP secured the most votes and it was the only Party that increased its percentage share of the votes over the 1961 election. However, the Governor refused to comply with British conventions that would have allowed Dr. Cheddi Jagan to form the government as the leader of the Party with the majority of votes. Instead, the Governor through a constitutional amendment called on Mr. Forbes Burnham of the People's National Congress (PNC) to institute a government with the assistance of the UF (United Force) creating the short-lived PNC-UF Coalition.

The December 7, 1964 date is strategic in that it represents the climax of international intrigue to remove a popular government from office, a government elected through free, fair, and transparent elections right on from 1953. It is significant to note that the PPP on several occasions has been the victim of reduced terms in office, culminating in aborted policy formulation and implementation, e.g., in the 1953, 1961, and 1997 terms.

Early Efforts to Remove the PPP

But the focus here is to show how in 1964 we reached the point where the PPP Government's term of office was aborted and an election slated for December 7. Universal Adult Suffrage was introduced in 1953 when the PPP won the national election. The local middle class, a hodgepodge of the league of Colored People (LCP) and the British Guiana East Indian Association (BEGEIA), etc., secured only 13% of the vote. Engaging in a strong alliance with the colonial elite, this local middle class (LCP, BGEIA, etc.) made strong use of the Communist threat in the Region, aided and abetted by the PPP. Britain subsequently suspended the Constitution after the PPP Government was in office for only 133 days.

The U.S. Special National Intelligence Estimate on March 21, 1961 alluded in its report to the PPP's communist ideology and its closeness to Castro's Cuba and Moscow. Britain, under constant U.S. pressure, was not prepared to grant Independence under Jagan, but it could not remove the PPP under the then electoral system. The U.S. Government and less so the British perceived the PPP as a Communist threat to the Region.

U.S. Secretary of State Rusk in a telegram to Lord Home expressed concern over a Jagan victory in the August 21, 1961 election. The U.S. Government tried to stop the 1961 election and remove Jagan simultaneously. Part of the telegram on August 11, 1961 reads as:

. . . No doubt you would expect us to show considerable sensitivity about the prospect of Castroism in the Western Hemisphere and that we are not inclined to give people like Jagan the same benefit of the doubt which was given two or three years ago to Castro himself. However, we do believe that Jagan and his American wife are very far to the left indeed and that his accession to power in British Guiana would be a most troublesome setback in this Hemisphere.

President Kennedy and Prime Minister Macmillan in a Memorandum of Conversation at Birch Grove, England June 30, 1963, detailed the recommendation for a Burnham-D'Aguiar coalition and the need to institute PR. Clearly, the U.S. stage-managed the birth of a PNC-UF Coalition long before the 1964 elections. The U.S., true to form, ensured that democracy, freedom, and due process play second fiddle to consolidation of its capitalist interests.

Political instability and racial tension turned out to be important conditions that aided the U.S. and British Governments to rid them of the PPP Administration. The 1962-1964 disturbances constituted the foreign-instigated violence, manifested not only through overt action of British troops, but also through the covert interventions of the Central Intelligence Agency (CIA). Some covert CIA operations included utilizing proxy groups as the Trade Union Council, opposition political groups, and the church. These disturbances left 700 people dead by 1964.

Class Interests

For those who believe that local and foreign class interests were not implicated in these disturbances think again. Guyana then was an underdeveloped dependent country within a capitalist world economy. Therefore, the foreign interventionists while primarily geared toward preventing the formation of a satellite communist state, simultaneously protected and consolidated their own capitalist interests.

Thus, we saw opposition to the Kaldor Budget by big business interests politically discernible in the UF and in the middle class penetration of the PNC by such right-wing parties as the National Democratic Party. The Kaldor Budget was intended to meet the working-class needs. In short, foreign interventionists wanted to place big business' representatives in political power.

The PNC-UF coalition was middle class in brand name. In 1968, the PNC kicked the UF out of the Coalition. The PNC then commenced the class fabrication process where a new propertied ownership class, a product of politics and not economics, was born. The PNC elite had now taken birth.

Class & Race

The December 1964 elections brought to a temporary conclusion the battle between Capitalism/Right Orientation and Communism/Left Orientation. But it still left unresolved the problem of the linkage between class, race and ethnicity in Guyana. Jagan believes that Indians and Africans are not a uni-class, implying that class, race and ethnicity are interrelated and interactive. Rodney argues that the dominant role of racial division is tawdry. Perry Mars commenting on the disturbances in the 1960s noted the importance of class and class relations in political change.

The U.S. dominated the stage-managed efforts aimed at removing the PPP from the political scene from 1953 through 1964. The rationale for this kind of American imperial conquest has to do with supporting the gains of American capitalism globally and that these gains are more important than national sovereignty. The bottom line for the U.S. is that Communism is a threat to capitalism.

At any rate, the December 1964 elections symbolizes a reversal of democracy and due process in local politics as well as a betrayal of trust in international relations.

Compelling Evidence Supports the 1997 Election Results

The People's Progressive Party/Civic (PPP/C) won the 1997 general election. The December 15 election results were known to each political party, through their polling agents immediately after the polls were closed. Hugh Desmond Hoyte's response in refusing to accept the election outcome, was not because he primarily disagreed with the results. But because he wanted to continue as Leader of the People's National Congress (PNC).

Calling PNC supporters to the streets constituted 'muscle flexing' to demonstrate that he still had the capacity to mobilize the PNC rank and file. In his judgment, the ongoing street protests added credibility to his leadership.

Hoyte knew that two successive electoral defeats, and growing inroads made by the PPP/C into Region 4, a PNC stronghold, could spell the end of him as Leader of the PNC. The December 15 aftermath was publicly perceived, then, as Hoyte's last stand.

The PNC's refusal to accept the results was further weakened by the international observers' approbation of the electoral process. Here is a shopping list of some comments from international and local agencies.

The International observers validated the integrity of the December 1997 election results. These organizations included the International Foundation for Election Systems (IFES), Organization of American States (OAS), and the Commonwealth Observer Group. The Electoral Assistance Bureau (EAB) was the local observer team.

- George Jones, IFES Director of Programs for the Americas and a former U.S. Ambassador to Guyana, praised the General Elections Commission (GEC) and its Chairman Doodnauth Singh said that "Chairman Singh and the GEC are to be commended for their professionalism and success in holding an election of which all Guyanese should be proud."

- The IFES team applauded many aspects of the election process, including accuracy of the voter lists; clearly-defined, secret voting procedures at each polling station; and the non-intrusive presence of security personnel at each polling station. The 8-person IFES team unanimously concluded that the December 15, 1997 election results were clean, orderly and peaceful.

- Another international observer team was the OAS with 28 election observers representing 10 countries. Head of the team was OAS Assistant Secretary General Ambassador Christopher Thomas a press statement, he said that he was "satisfied that the elections commission worked with great care and attention to assure that all citizens of Guyana were given an opportunity to cast their vote."

- The December 1997 election results were supported by the U.S., Canada, Brazil, Colombia, Venezuela, and El Salvador, through their representatives at the OAS.

- Former Tanzanian President Ali Hassan Mwinyi led a 14-member Commonwealth Observer Group to Guyana to observe the December 1997 election. This Group definitively stated that "As a result of our observations on polling day, we concluded that the voters were freely able to express their will." The Commonwealth Observers applauded the GEC on their preparations for the elections.

- A local group, the EAB, recruited and trained 1,100 local observers for the elections. In an interim statement, the EAB declared that "the procedures employed at the polls as reflecting impartiality...voting was done in an unrestricted manner, with the secrecy of the ballot not being compromised." The EAB enforced the integrity and transparency of the elections, thus, "EAB considers the results of the count observed at the polling places as having represented the will of the Guyanese voters . . . December 15 was undoubtedly the best polling day witnessed in the past three decades, and was an election of which all concerned could be proud."

- James Foley, Deputy Spokesman for the U.S. Department of State, congratulated Guyanese on the success of national elections held in December 1997.Foley added that "We note with satisfaction the improvements that were made in the electoral process in Guyana congratulate the independent Elections Commission and the nongovernmental observers and organizers whose presence helped ensure the transparency of this process."

- Further, the U.S. Department of State 1999 Country Reports on Human Rights Practices indicated that Guyanese voted in free, fair, and nonviolent elections in December 1997.

CARICOM remained silent for 24 years, as the totalitarian regime exploited the last vestiges of human dignity of the Guyanese people. It certainly was encouraging in 1998 to receive CARICOM's intervention at a crucial juncture in our history, as democracy was given a new lease of life. CARICOM's intervention via the Herdmanston Accord came in the wake of sporadic street violence confined to only a few streets in Georgetown, and coming, too, on the heels of the December 1997 election results. The two main parties (PPP/C and PNC) reached a settlement through the Herdmanston Accord and, later, the St. Lucia Statement.

- The Herdmanston Accord, inter alia, made provisions for the conduct of an independent international audit, to be administered by CARICOM.CARICOM, subsequently, concluded the audit, declaring that the results were free and fair. The audit, also, did not uncover any padded voters' lists in favor of the PPP/Civic, or any other political party. The Leader of the Minority Party, later called for an audit of the Audit.

- It is worth noting that former CARICOM Chairman and former Prime Minister of St. Vincent and the Grenadines Sir James

Mitchell, said that the 5-year term of the Guyana Government should not have been reduced, given that the CARICOM Audit of the 1997 national polls determined that the ballots were reasonably free from contamination.

Clearly, the December 1997 national election results were reliable and valid, given the intense scrutiny exercised over the elections process through international and local observers, political party agents, the verification process of which the PNC representatives walked out, and the CARICOM audit. While few administrative glitches occurred, they, however, were not sufficiently significant in themselves to alter the final outcome of the election.

Some racist and misplaced broadcasters arrogantly call daily for the PPP/C to demit office on January 17, 2001.They would, in the name of balance and objectivity, do well for the broadcast journalism profession, by also at the same time reinforce the current work of the all-party committee in its pursuit of an appropriate governance process after January 17.

These broadcast journalists, if they really are journalists, should know, too, that Hoyte refused to accept the results of the CARICOM Audit, by calling for an audit of the Audit.

The Herdmanston Accord states "The Parties to this Accord will accept the findings of the first stage of the audit as binding upon them . . . in the first stage, an urgent review of the due process of the count on and after 15 December 1997 (including the role of the Elections Commission) to be completed within three months of 17 January 1998 with a view to ascertainment of the votes cast for the respective political parties. . . ." The Leader of the Minority Party, clearly, did not accept the Audit results as required by the Herdmanston Accord.

Given the election results and the Audit findings of the December 1997 election, we cannot, then, seek to change the election rules, with the view to altering its outcome to one's advantage where a defeat becomes converted to a victory.

Journalists have, largely, ignored the unscrupulous challenges made to the elections process in the period immediately following the election. Those misguided media operatives have to take responsibility for the temporary mayhem created in the aftermath of the December political outcome.

The burden of creating a new environment in the spirit of the Herdmanston Accord, must firmly be placed within the work parameters of broadcast and print journalists, especially in an age of sophisticated information technology. Poor journalists make for a poor environment!!

Redundant Elections Brouhaha

Dreariness appears to punctuate the lives of many seeming politicians between elections; and perhaps, for them the election season becomes the threshold for that much-needed excitement; elections bouts are stirring times; moments when the elusive personal recognition becomes a glorious goal; and when opportunities abound for political muscle-flexing; and for what purposes? Certainly, these numerous political posturing in recent months can't be good for consolidating a fragile democracy.

Recently, I spoke about the elections process as a travesty; I said the following: "Self-interest, not the people's interests have marred the political life of this nation; the constant humbug of unscrupulous demands for changes in electoral rules and systems, the relentless and selfish haggling over shared governance; the predictable election writs; unyielding bickering over constitutional reform; media distortions; the race card; and yes, the street protests, among others, are what we have come to expect during an election season. But the people have the power to end this political nuisance, a political tragedy in some sense."

Now there is more. A first PNCR's request extending the Claims and Objections (C&O) period; request granted. Now a PNCR's second request appears for more extension of the C&O period.

Meanwhile in Region 2 on the Essequibo Coast, the PNCR's objections to some names have turned out to be groundless; some of the names are: Ramrattie Babulall, Lall Bachan Singh, Bohan Singh, etc.

Recall in 2001 the PNC's published list of voters showing that that list of voters did not exist; but their names appeared on the Voters' List; PPP scrutineers then quickly discovered 80% of those voters that the PNC claimed did not exist.

Objections are appropriate in order for any elections process to achieve integrity; but such objections must have a foundation; and the current reported PNCR's national multi-objections also must have a basis in fact. However, current revelations suggest that many PNCR's objections seem to be groundless. This behavior is not good for consolidating democracy.

And the PNCR still wants house-to-house verification to sanitize the 2006 Preliminary Voters' List (PVL). The 2006 PVL has a direct lineage to the 2001 list, based on house-to-house registration completed in 1996-1997; and scrutinized by the governing and opposition parties. The PNC subsequently claimed that this 1997 voters' lists were padded. A CARICOM Audit team concluded that it did not discover a single fraudulent ballot in the 1997 Elections.

Former GECOM Chairman Joe Singh had provided UNDP with a duplicate of the 2001 Official List of Electors (OLE) database for safe-keeping; a comparison of the GECOM data base with the UNDP database was made; GECOM's IT department in association with IDEA IT expert and with the political parties in attendance, opened the UNDP-held database; the Cyclic Redundancy Checksum (CRC) used for data validation indicated that the GECOM 2001 database was unaltered.

Notwithstanding the CRC validation, the PNCR maintained its criticisms against the 2001 OLE database. GECOM then invited Mr. Vedove, a Swiss electoral expert, to review the PNCR's complaints; he found no evidence that the database was violated. Then the PNCR demanded the application of biometrics; but GECOM's database already includes the following biometric features: a photograph; signature; hair color; eye color; and distinguishing marks, reinforced through claims and objections, fingerprint scanning, and cross-referencing exercise.

In addition, the Electoral Assistance Bureau (EAB) has reported identifying 85% of voters from its random voters' list, adding integrity to the 2001 OLE as well as the 2006 PVL.

International observers also validated the integrity of the 1997 OLE and the election results. Their observations now follow:

- James Foley, Deputy Spokesman for the U.S. Department of State, congratulated Guyanese on the success of national elections held in December 1997. Foley added that "We note with satisfaction the improvements that were made in the electoral process in Guyana. We congratulate the independent Elections Commission and the non-governmental observers and organizers whose presence helped ensure the transparency of this process."

- Further, the U.S. Department of State 1999 Country Reports on Human Rights Practices indicated that Guyanese voted in free, fair, and nonviolent elections in December 1997.

- George Jones, IFES Director of Programs for the Americas and a former U.S. Ambassador to Guyana, praised the General Elections Commission (GEC) and its Chairman Doodnauth Singh, thus: "Chairman Singh and the GEC are to be commended for their professionalism and success in holding an election of which all Guyanese should be proud."

- The IFES team applauded many aspects of the election process, including accuracy of the voter lists; clearly-defined, secret voting procedures at each polling station; and the non-intrusive presence of security personnel at each polling station. The 8-person IFES team unanimously concluded that the December 15, 1997 election results were clean, orderly and peaceful.

- Head of the OAS team Assistant Secretary General Ambassador Christopher Thomas said that he was "satisfied that the elections commission worked with great care and attention to assure that all citizens of Guyana were given an opportunity to cast their vote."

- The December 1997 election results were supported by the U.S., Canada, Brazil, Colombia, Venezuela, and El Salvador.

- Former Tanzanian President Ali Hassan Mwinyi with a 14-member Commonwealth Observer Group to Guyana definitively stated that "As a result of our observations on polling day, we concluded that the voters were freely able to express their will." The Commonwealth Observers applauded the GEC on their preparations for the elections.

- A local group, the EAB, in an interim statement, declared that "the procedures employed at the polls as reflecting impartiality . . . voting was done in an unrestricted manner, with the secrecy of the ballot not being compromised." The EAB enforced the integrity and transparency of the elections, thus, "EAB considers the results of the count observed at the polling places as having represented the will of the Guyanese voters . . . December 15 was undoubtedly the best polling day witnessed in the past three decades, and was an election of which all concerned could be proud."

- The CARICOM Audit of the 1997 national polls determined that the ballots were reasonably free from contamination.

Abundant sanitization evidence confirms the integrity of the 1997 and 2001 OLEs, and indeed the 2006 PLV. independent GECOM has a responsibility to execute; GECOM's responsibility is to end this perpetual redundant elections mêlée.

Why Worry about Brain Drain, when there can be 'Brain Circulation'

Some pen pushers seem to have a divine right of daily bringing sorry tidings to the people; would it not be good if we can have this every day errand interspersed with a goodie, at least intermittently? People are beginning to see through these stringers' outpourings, fast redefining them as irrelevant through imbalance and fundamental unfairness in their messages.

Not too long ago, the report that 86% of graduates are emigrants has become an important pastime and exudes considerable excitement for some. This 86% was perhaps the 'brain drain' exclusive story intended to shock the pants and panties out of this nation. Well, it did not. And I will be surprised if it did; the brain drain phenomenon has been a recurring decimal throughout the 20th century in different parts of the globe. In fact, the 20th century is described as the century of refugees; the century of migration.

The rate of Guyanese emigration has always shown a steady rise since the early 1950s. Official statistics show that 32,000 persons emigrated between 1960 and 1970; and about 10,000 persons per year emigrated within the 1975-79 period. Between 1969 and 1976, 48,639 Guyanese migrated overseas, with 40.8% to the U.S., 30.7% to Canada, and 11.3% to the United Kingdom.

We know about costs and benefits of immigration labor for the host countries, and costs and benefits of emigration to the countries of origin; One view suggests that the loss of skilled talent from developing countries exacts a great cost to those countries; prompting Bhagwati to propose a tax on skilled emigrants, referred to as the Bhagwati tax; another perspective shows that emigration from developing to developed economies can produce a win-win situation; skilled people living in the Diaspora can make a big difference to their countries of origin; we need to make this win-win happen.

The emigration rates of skilled workers of Guyana, Suriname, Jamaica, and Haiti were in excess of 80% in 2000; the Philippines, India, and China have 1,260,879, 1,012,613, and 906,337, respectively; the largest pool of overseas talent, huge diasporas.

The World Bank notes that 8 out of 10 Haitians and Jamaicans with college degrees live overseas; and in excess of 50% of university-educated professionals from Central America and the Caribbean live overseas.

The Global Economic Prospects 2006, a World Bank publication, indicates that about 200 million people live outside of their home countries; their remittances totaling about US$225 billion in 2005; a tremendous booster for poverty alleviation.

Anyway, it's good that we have Balasubramanyam and Wei of the University of Lancaster, bearers of good tidings, amid the shocking news of 86% of our graduates fleeing Guyana; they propose that the rate of return to a unit of investment by the diaspora may be greater than that of the traditional foreign direct investment (FDI).

Therefore, we now have to locate the Non-Resident Guyanese (NRGs), especially those in the U.S., Canada, and the United Kingdom, if we are to economically transform Guyana. India and China thrive on their diasporas. Why can't Guyana? How can NRGs help?

It's more than remittances; Guyana could develop policies that transform 'brain drain' into 'brain circulation'. Brain circulation networks are possible where overseas Guyanese can facilitate Guyana with scientists and Research and Development personnel; business start-ups; and a network of professionals attached to multinational corporations. Some of these types of brain circulation already may be a reality; already producing some benefits to Guyana. Of what good would NRGs be to Guyana?

NRGs can make technology and know-how available to Guyana; in the same way that Indian software firms outsource with diaspora firms in the U.S., Guyanese companies could strive to effect business arrangements with Guyanese diaspora firms.

NRGs can make direct investments to Guyana; again, the Ides of March may not know, but some diaspora packaging investments have arrived; perhaps, the beginnings of diaspora joint ventures or acquisitions.

NRGs' involvement in Guyana may be guided not only by the profit motive, but by a genuine desire for establishing and sustaining a base in their country of origin.

NRGs through a sustained engagement in their country of origin may in the end reduce permanent migration.

But NRGs have to be mobilized; the talent that emigrates is not completely lost to the sending country; we need to intensify the creation of brain circulation networks; and stop brooding over brain drain.

New Global Human Order, Globally Recognized

Former President Cheddi Jagan died on March 6, 1997 at 12:23 a.m. at Walter Reed Army Medical Center in the United States of America. Dr. Jagan bequeathed several legacies for the Guyanese people, but a significant birthright, among others, was his lifelong concern to bring happiness to the working class.

Today, this enduring concern has become the foundation for his globally-recognized legacy, the New Global Human Order (NGHO); Dr. Jagan formally initiated the NGHO's principles in 1996; principles that already were totally enshrined in Jagan's political life; principles that speak to eliminating poverty among the working class, not only in Guyana but also in the developing world; principles that speak to giving the market economy a makeover, a human face. Jagan, for the first time since 1992 clearly, outlined his philosophic vision for Guyana in a speech in 1996 to the International Conference on the Global Human Order. What he presented was quite provocative for the squeamish, but practical, and required endorsement and implementation; endorsement he got in abundance. The view of the NGHO is remarkable, aimed at revitalizing poor developing nations through a just and fair partnership with the developed world.

Jagan's vision of a developmental strategy incorporating NGHO's principles focuses on the relationship of the worker to the products of his labor; on the process of producing that product; and rewards that flow to workers and to developing economies; NGHO's principles only becoming a reality if there is a blending of the market economy with governmental interventions in both North and South; the U.S. does this quite well.

In the Epilogue to the last Edition of The West On Trial, Jagan explained why a new global human order was necessary and where anything less was insufficient, thus: "Market-driven economic globalization and unbridled modernization . . . are leading to a spiral of marginalization and exclusion. . . ."

The social and economic divisions between the advantaged and the disadvantaged in the industrialized nations of the North, in the developing and underprivileged countries of the South, and differences in accomplishments between North and South, are expanding. Clearly, the fight to eliminate poverty and restore human dignity has to be waged across national borders. Dr. Jagan knew all along that the fight for Guyana's freedom was intertwined in the fight for world freedom, and so he took his battle against poverty and hunger to the international fora; a North and South working together as partners. This perspective, according to Dr. Jagan, would eliminate advanced nations' stranglehold on developing countries. But the World Trade Organization (WTO) is a brake on removing this iron grip. How?

Under the General Agreement on Tariffs and Trade (GATT), the capacity of governments to control businesses and their economies, largely is conceded to the WTO and transnational corporations. GATT, in setting up the WTO in 1995, was not so much concerned with regulating trade, as to place individual governments under the control of private capital without a human face. Some examples of the WTO's excesses follow.

The 120 countries that are signatories to GATT must reduce tariffs, stop farm subsidies, treat foreign corporations the same as the local corporations, comply with all corporate patent claims, and heed the decisions of the WTO which has the authority to enforce these agreements through trade sanctions. The GATT agreement, in establishing the WTO, needs reexamination against a background of high levels of poverty in developing economies. Implementing the NGHO and maintaining democracy in countries with a fragile democracy become problematic if the GATT agreement is not reconsidered and reconfigured for poor nations.

Implementing the NGHO requires a level of international cooperation and reorientation of ideological thrusts that have never before been seen. Most advanced industrial nations are solely motivated by the pursuit of profit and rapid capital accumulation.

The NGHO may be more feasible in a mixed economic system with both capitalist and interventionist principles rather than within a sole capitalist economic system. This mix is scarce on the international scene.

The following developments attest to Jagan's resilience and fortitude in his aggressive promotion of the NGHO: appeal to world leaders in 1994 arguing the case for a new order where the predominance of human development becomes the guideline for action; paper presented for the UN-sponsored World Hearings on Development, 1994; paper presented to the European Commission, 1994; paper presented to the Inter-Sessional CARICOM Heads of Government in St. Vincent and the Grenadines 1994; address to the Commonwealth Heads of Government in New Zealand, 1995; letter to the President of the World Bank, 1996; paper presented at the Global Development Initiative Advisory Group at the Carter Centre, 1996; address to the World Food Summit in Rome, 1996; Memorandum disseminated at the hemispheric Summit on Sustainable Development in Bolivia, 1996.

The Guyana Parliament in 1994 approved a resolution on the NGHO. In 1996, an international conference on the NGHO took place, culminating in its endorsement; and with endorsements in 1997 from CARICOM, The Group of

77 and China (G 77), and the UN General Assembly. The UN General Assembly has now debated Dr. Jagan's NGHO.

The late President explained the complexion and nature of the NGHO, thus: "To attain a new Global Human Order, it is necessary to establish a sound and just system of global governance based on: a genuine North/South partnership and interdependence for mutual benefit; a democratic culture of representative, consultative and participatory democracy and a lean and clean administration; a people-centered development strategy free from external domination; application of science and technology for increased production and productivity; and the creation of a Global Development Fund."

To squander the opportunity to put the NGHO in place is to condemn humanity to a lifetime of despair, alienation, and hopelessness; in short, a lifetime of poverty and hunger; a lifetime of nothingness; no need for this wastage.

Trumanizing the New Global Human Order

The New Global Human Order (NGHO) made its formal appearance in the theater of politics in the 1990s. But the essence of the NGHO was birthed as long ago as 1945 when Dr. Jagan's political mission included poverty elimination and advancing a human-centered development among the developed and developing economies; this is what the NGHO is all about.

Last week, I talked about the NGHO's principles and its numerous endorsements, both regionally and internationally. Today, let's review its current status.

A Resolution on the NGHO was tabled on November 29, 2000 before the United Nations General Assembly, and after that adopted through a consensus. It took six (6) years of campaigning for the NGHO proposal to reach the United Nations documentation and consciousness.

Many previous attempts at introducing different international development paradigms achieved approval; but their implementations have always met with opposition. The UN approved these two Declarations: Program of Action for a New International Economic Order; and Declaration on International Economic Cooperation 1990; with little or no implementation. Then there were the global summit conferences between 1990 and 1995 on children; population and development; sustainable development of small states, human settlements and food, among others. Subsequently, the UN documented an Agenda for development and an Agenda for Peace; again with minimum results.

The success then of the NGHO seems daunting, given the sterile results from the UN Declarations, summits, and agendas of the past decades; to advance the NGHO agenda to a threshold of implementation requires political will and financial resources. Countries of both North and South will need to collectively accept and these requirements as the way forward; and then forge ahead toward the implementation phase.

Clearly, the developed nations continue to be the bugbear in implementing something as useful as the NGHO.

Fighting for Real Independence

The month of March is the Cheddi Jagan month when we celebrate the life and times of Dr. Cheddi Jagan, former President of Guyana. History will remember Cheddi Jagan as a world leader; who struggled for social progress among the dispossessed and the disadvantaged; who vigorously implanted progressive political thought; who was a resolute builder of political movements; who forged the political-labor nexus; who was an unwavering Caribbean integrationist; who was a true internationalist in his unrelenting promulgation of the New Global Human Order; and whose authentic local legacy has to be his tireless fight for national unity, working-class unity, and racial unity. His ideas and his indefatigable promotion of these ideas have not only redefined the Caribbean, but have impacted the world of the poor.

The fight against colonial hegemony to achieve *Independence*, working together for *national unity*, working-class unity, and racial unity, and the promulgation of the *New Global Human Order* are only a few of the major thrusts of Dr. Jagan's work. But today, I want to focus on his fight for Independence.

The former President of Guyana was a tenacious fighter for Independence; and he is among the first few to have kicked off this struggle against colonial domination. This novel idea of Independence emerged in 1945 in a Dr. Cheddi Jagan's pamphlet titled **COOPERATIVE WAY**.

The PPP birthed in 1950 continued from where the Political Affairs Committee (PAC) left off; unrelenting agitation for Independence became the number one item on the PPP's agenda; demands included universal adult suffrage, a fully elected legislature, a Cabinet of elected Ministers, etc. This feverish campaigning drew the ire of British planters, prompting the arrival of the Waddington Commission; this was a small victory for the PPP struggle against colonial hegemony; a struggle that conceived and gave birth to universal adult suffrage; a struggle that designed the road map for Independence.

The first election under universal adult suffrage happened in 1953 during the Cold War. Not long after, the Colonial Office removed the PPP Government after only 133 days in office; the spread of communism in Guyana topped the list of the British and American Governments' reasons for the ouster.

Proper scrutiny of the PPP Government's Parliamentary measures were all working-class based, and not communistic; the removal had to do with American and British vested economic interests, interests quite attuned to the Truman and the Lyttleton Doctrines.

The Colonial Office, dumbstruck by PPP's enthusiastic campaigning, agreed to initiate dialog, not primarily for negotiating Independence, principally for blocking PPP's return to power; hence the 1960 London Constitutional Conference. The People's National Congress showed little enthusiasm for immediate Independence in 1960.

In 1962, to further delay Independence, the PNC conditioned the bestowal of Independence with a change in the electoral system. Great Britain eventually granted Independence to Guyana on May 26, 1966. Vernon Nunes while in detention at Sibley Hall, penned "INDEPENDENCE YES! CELEBRATIONS NO!" a front-page caption in Thunder of April 1966.

Dr. Jagan advanced these reasons for not celebrating Independence: (1) the colonial Constitution did not protect fundamental rights, a pre-condition for national unity; (2) the colonialists' marionettes gained power through a rigged constitutional arrangement; (3) detention without trial was still the order of the day;(4) colonialists still exerted political and economic domination via firming up the economy rooted in primary production and extraction, and the escalating debt burdens; (5) the state of emergency was still in place to silence and bully the working class; (6) PPP comrades were still languishing in detention at Sibley Hall.

The British political authorities in an unabashed show of imperialist intrigue with their American counterparts granted Independence in 1966, not because they loved the Guyanese people; but because of a concerted effort to: keep Dr. Jagan and the PPP out of office; consolidate British and American vested interests; demonstrate the virility of the Truman and Lyttleton Doctrine; infuse the 'American way'; and illustrate, unwittingly and unintentionally perhaps, the meaning of political opportunism.

The PPP's election victory in 1992 cemented the way for real Independence, prompting Dr. Jagan to proclaim that the people have won and ". . .that for the first time since independence, we have a Parliament which is truly representative of the people. . . ." This year marks the 40th Independence anniversary; and for the first time in these last few years, a new spirit of real Independence has stalked this land; and to recapture the spirit of 1953 which is national unity, working-class unity, and racial unity, may very well require an engaging public discourse and consensus. That's what Dr. Cheddi Jagan represents and what he means to this nation.

Marginalization of Guyana's Working Class

The experience of marginalization/social exclusion touches large numbers of people across the globe, people of different colors, ethnicity, age, and gender. The experience of social exclusion is located in countries of both the core and periphery of the world system. Advanced economic development then is no guarantee against marginalization; poor economic development breeds poverty and creates vulnerable groups. Denmark is one of those countries in the world with the lowest level of social and economic inequality; yet Denmark has problems of integrating some groups into the labor market. Globalization, a political tool of the powerful nations, can marginalize an entire society, a globalization that favors the core countries to the disadvantage of countries in the periphery. And a dominant group can marginalize certain classes/ethnicities in a society, too.

Identifying risk factors for marginalization is a useful preventive strategy. Significant risk factors for marginalization include poverty, unemployment, sickness, physical disability; risk factors are not forms of marginalization and their presence should not be equated with marginalization. There is an erroneous perception that interprets risk factors for marginalization and marginalization itself as being synonymous. In Denmark, a marginalization pattern has persisted, notwithstanding improved economic conditions in the labor market in the 1990s. Indeed, marginalization could persist, despite prevailing good employment conditions. What about Guyana?

There is a view in Guyana that protestors intermittently take to the streets because they feel marginalized. And there are some who believe that the current People's Progressive Party/Civic (PPP/C) Administration should accept some responsibility for supposed African marginalization. The People's National Congress (PNC) marginalized both the African and Indian working class in its ruling heydays between 1968 and 1992, another view. Still a further view is that poverty and unemployment are synonymous with marginalization, albeit erroneous. However, poverty fills the lives of urban Africans; Indians, Amerindians, and Africans in that order experience poverty in rural locales. But poverty by itself is not sufficient to marginalize any population group. Many poor societies demonstrate that their poor are quite well integrated, true only when experiences of inequality are about the same for all. An ORSTOM report[1] notes that in countries of the South, "the poor remain incorporated within family and extra-family networks of social protection and mutual assistance, this incorporation produces integration and not exclusion." Unemployment and poverty, however, are significant risk factors for marginalization; but they are not one and the same as marginalization.

The PNC Party recorded a history of defeats at all democratically-held elections since 1957. Between 1968 and 1985, the Party took political power through dubious means, rigged elections. But even those rigged elections results demanded some kind of credibility and sustainability, in order to garner some posturing of legitimacy. Using a racist spin to rationalize the rigged elections for legitimacy purposes, the PNC reinstated a competing and conflictful inter-ethnic grassroots base; applying a competing race card was the answer, with education and economic institutions exploited as the main conduits.

On the education side, the community high school and the multilateral secondary school were birthed, notwithstanding their lower status than the existing elite high schools. However, their initial locations impugned their integrity as a novel and innovative concept in education. Both types of school were distributed

---

[1] Poverty, Unemployment and Exclusion in the Countries of the South: Reflections from the Royaumont Seminar as a Contribution to the Work of the World Summit on Social Development (Paris: ORSTOM, 1995), p. 7.

according to a racial pattern, initially located only in neighborhoods where Africans predominated.

Further, multilateral and community high school leavers' competition for jobs was practically non-existent; the occupational structure, by absorbing personnel from mainly elite high schools, sealed the fate of those working-class youngsters from both multilaterals and community highs.

Racial distribution of community highs and multilaterals and non-competitiveness of those school leavers for jobs increased the utility value of the race card; the notion was creating rivalry between working-class Indians and Africans. In the end, both Indian and African students as well as the Indian and African working-class became victims.

On the economic side, clearly, predominantly African PNC elite dominated and marginalized its own working-class supporters, including other working class people; but this was the PNC's method of consolidating its power base. The PNC elite was born in the post-Independence period. After Independence, the PNC's middle class became the new elite. This elite retained the structures of colonial domination and exploitation, including the preservation of an expanding colonial bureaucracy, the beginnings of the PNC's elite power base, its evolution into a comprador class with ties to international capitalism, abandonment of a national agenda, and unequal distribution of resources to the working and lower classes (Hintzen).

Hintzen argues that the PNC elite also inflicted social and economic damage on those Africans and Coloreds, formerly of the middle class in the colonial struggle; those who subsequently fell from grace. In this context, the PNC elite's response to sustaining their levers of political, economic, and military power was color blind. Working people of all ethnic groups, including other groups opposed to PNC rule became victims of this internal human savagery. And class not race became relevant to the PNC elite's world view to protect their power base.

As became clearer, the PNC Administration not only advanced ethnic division through education. It showed spectacular success with creating the African elite. The PNC elite, a relatively small group of people, wielded political, economic, and military power. The three areas of power—political, economic, and military—were interlocking, in that decisions in one area impacted the other two areas, and the elite members in all three areas were interchangeable. The African elite was the power elite in Guyana during PNC rule.

PNC Party paramountcy further strengthened this elite's power base. PNC working-class supporters never shared nor became part of this power design. The PNC working class' sole utility value was to act as the Party's grassroots base, an electoral buffer to the Indian working-class, provided some semblance of sustainability and temporary legitimacy to the illegal PNC Government.

Social Marginalization & Ethnicity
An Update

The experience of marginalization touches large numbers of people across the globe, people of different classes, colors, ethnicity, age, and gender. The experience of social exclusion is located in countries of both the core and periphery of the world system. Advanced economic development then is no guarantee against marginalization; poor economic development breeds poverty and creates vulnerable groups. Denmark is one of those countries in the world with the lowest level of social and economic inequality; yet Denmark has problems of integrating some groups into the labor market. Globalization, a political tool of the powerful nations, can marginalize an entire society, a globalization that favors the core countries to the disadvantage of countries in the periphery. And a dominant group can marginalize certain classes/ethnicities in a society, too.

Identifying risk factors for marginalization is a useful preventive strategy. Significant risk factors for marginalization include poverty, unemployment, sickness, physical disability; risk factors are not forms of marginalization and their presence should not be equated with marginalization. There is an erroneous perception that treats risk factors as marginalization. In Denmark, a marginalization pattern has persisted, notwithstanding improved economic conditions in the labor market in the 1990s. Indeed, marginalization could persist, despite prevailing good employment conditions.

Research studies in Denmark[1] define marginalization "as a process where there is a more or less comprehensive involuntary exclusion from participation in one or more spheres of life. A process where there is a normative expectation of participation both as regards the individual and in relation to the given socially dominant norms and practice."

The Denmark studies [2] see marginalization as a process, not as a condition; the individual can experience marginalization in some parts of the life cycle and not in other parts. Marginalization is an undesirable process for any person. Marginalization points to sections of society where expectations for participation of a person have to comply with the dominant system's beliefs, values, and norms. This means that it may be hard to differentiate between voluntary and involuntary marginalization; cases may exist where an individual makes a voluntary choice that may involuntarily produce marginalization; or where an individual makes progressive adaptations to his marginalized status and sees the experience as acceptable.

Marginalization involves exclusion from participation in some areas of society; this kind of participation is involuntary and incomplete; here both society and the individual expect participation to occur; but both society and the individual may have different expectations about the levels of participation required.

It is important to note that marginalization in one area of social life does not necessarily produce marginalization in others. Simmel [3]explains that marginalization is incomplete participation; Simmel notes that the poor are not necessarily marginalized.

Indian & African Marginalization

Let's now review some historical findings under the People's National Congress (PNC) regime. The PNC recorded a history of defeats at all democratically-held elections since 1957. Between 1968 and 1985, the Party took political power through dubious means, rigged elections. But even those rigged elections demanded some kind of credibility and sustainability, in order to garner some posturing of legitimacy. Using a racist spin to rationalize the rigged elections for legitimacy purposes, the PNC masterminded a competing and conflictful inter-ethnic grassroots base; the African/Indian race card was the answer; the 'race' conduits mainly were education and economic institutions.

On the education side, the community high school and the multilateral secondary school as a new concept in education received top billing. However, their initial locations impugned the integrity of their top billing. Both types of school were distributed according to a racial pattern, located only in neighborhoods where Africans predominated.

Only six multilateral secondary schools were constructed at that time; they were unable to accommodate successful community high school students at the Secondary Schools Proficiency Examination (SSPE). 'No placement, no school' became the battle cry among successful SSPE students. The result was not surprisingly a high incidence of school dropouts. Aborting school life at both the community highs and multilaterals unquestionably marginalized the working-class of both major ethnic groups, Africans and Indians. Indian and African students outside the multilaterals' catchment neighborhoods came face to face with less opportunity for a placement in those six multilaterals. But more African than Indian students were placed in the six multilaterals, as those six multilaterals were established in African neighborhoods.

The worse was still to come. Multilateral and community high school leavers' competition for jobs was practically non-existent. The occupational structure drew its labor from elite high schools. Job non-competitiveness sealed the fate of these working-class youngsters from both the multilaterals and community highs. Their life chances and socioeconomic status were non-starters to any career consolidation.

The community and multilateral educational structures were and still are non-elite institutions. Their status was below that of the elite schools. The job market demanded elite education and that's what it got. Elite schools' outcomes were congruent to the demands and requirements of the job market. Working-class children mainly peopled community highs and multilaterals. The result, a streaming of schools, creating a division between schools mainly for elite children and schools essentially for workers' children, with elite children controlling the labor market.

Racial distribution of community highs and multilaterals and non-competitiveness of their school leavers for jobs aided the utility value of the race card; creating rivalry between working-class Indians and Africans. The PNC's strategy was as follows: having reinstated ethnic competition and conflict, the PNC's next step was to demonstrate to their working-class supporters through the race card that the other competing ethnic group threatened their livelihood; in any case, applying the race card secured temporary legitimacy for fraudulent elections. But in the end, both Indian and African students as well as the Indian and African working-class became victims.

Clearly, predominantly African PNC elite dominated and marginalized its own working-class supporters, including the Indian working class; but this was the PNC's method of consolidating its power base. After Independence, the PNC's middle class became the new elite. The elite retained the structures of colonial domination and exploitation, including the preservation of an expanding colonial bureaucracy,[4] the beginnings of the PNC's elite power base.

Hintzen[5] believed that African-Creole nationalism was the basis for struggle against colonial mobilization and colonial hegemony, simultaneously. But in the postcolonial period, African-Creole nationalism eventually subsided into neo-colonial control, abandoning the nationalist domestic agenda. The PNC elite became the comprador class tied to international capitalism. The comprador class refers to local elites who profit from the system of exploitation and whose interests become closely intertwined with their counterparts in the developed or metropolitan countries.[6] The PNC's comprador class reproduced itself through its connections with international capitalists and the world capitalist system.

Comprador activities meant an abandonment of domestic nationalism and a domestic agenda. The PNC elite frequently coerced and exploited its working-class supporters and other people on the lower rungs of the class ladder. These nefarious activities sustained the PNC elite's power base. The foundation was now laid to unequally distribute resources to all the working and lower classes, irrespective of race. The foundation for enhanced inequality was well established.

All working and lower classes were placed within caste structures, controlled by PNC power holders, in the end reducing their social mobility. The caste structure stagnated the social mobility of all working-class groups who were not part of the PNC as well as those working-class people who supported the PNC Party, but not linked to the comprador-class activities.

Hintzen[7] argues that the PNC elite also inflicted social and economic damage on those Africans and Coloreds, formerly of the middle class in the colonial struggle and who subsequently fell from grace. The PNC elite believed that the former African and Colored middle class posed a potential threat vis-à-vis their previous power position. In this context, the PNC elite's response to sustaining their levers of political, economic, and military power was color blind. Working people of all ethnic groups became victims of this internal human savagery. And class not race became relevant to the PNC elite's world view to protect their power base.

As became clearer, the PNC Administration not only advanced ethnic division through education. It showed spectacular success with creating the African elite. The PNC elite, a relatively small group of people, had political, economic, and military power. The elite used this power for their own benefit. The three areas of power—political, economic, and military—were interlocking, in that decisions in one area impacted the other two areas, and the elite members in all three areas were interchangeable.

The elite shared similar race, class and educational origins. The similarity in origins demonstrated that the elite knew each other, interacted socially, and was part of the inner circle of the PNC ruling class. The elite member accepted each other as equals; each saw the world with similar lens. The African elite became the power elite in Guyana during PNC rule.

PNC Party paramountcy further strengthened this elite's power base. PNC working-class supporters never shared nor became part of this power design. The PNC African working class' sole utility value was to act as that Party's grassroots base, as an electoral buffer to the Indian working-class, to provide some semblance of sustainability and temporary legitimacy to the illegal PNC Government. Under these conditions within the PNC ruling era, the Indian and African working class faced sustained inequality in accessing rewards to up-grade its life chances; it became marginalized.

Rationale

The purpose of this paper is to determine the participation levels of two major ethnic groups in Guyana—Indians and Africans—in the public sector, and to explain why some groups are successfully integrated and others are not. The findings may provide information on public policy formulation instrumental to helping groups at high risk of marginalization.

Marginalization studies have identified groups at high risk of marginalization; these are children, adolescents, ethnic minorities, persons with limited education, and mentally ill persons. Among these groups would be people who have coping capacity and others without, with regard to accessing the labor market.

In Guyana, a multiethnic society, who is marginalized? Are particular ethnic groups marginalized? Why marginalization? Is marginalization linked to the distribution of wealth? Is marginalization connected to a disintegration of bonds that make society cohesive? Do major ethnic groups have representative participation in the public sector? Answers to these questions would throw up strategies toward resolving political instability and will facilitate conflict resolution.

In Guyana, there is a view that protestors intermittently take to the streets because they feel marginalized. The main opposition party the People's National Congress Reform—One Guyana (PNCR–1G) shares this view. And there are some who believe that the current People's Progressive Party/Civic (PPP/C) Administration should accept some responsibility for perceived African marginalization. The PNC's policies, programs, and projects marginalized both the African and Indian working class in its ruling heydays between 1968 and 1992, another view.

An additional view includes the following: And some features of the Indo-Caribbean experience may very well add up to a profile in historical marginalization. These features include dislocation from India, massive burden of labor in the Caribbean, ethnic victimization in the post-colonial era, and migration to the metropolitan centers. Such characteristics generate a double marginalization, as Naipaul[8] would say. First, there is marginalization via their relationship to a Euro-centered Creole culture. Second, there is marginalization via their 'outsider' status as Indians in the Caribbean.

Still a further view is that poverty and unemployment are synonymous with marginalization, albeit erroneous. However, poverty fills the lives of urban Africans; but Indians, Amerindians, and Africans in that order experience poverty in rural locales. And poverty by itself is not sufficient to marginalize any population group. Many poor societies demonstrate that their poor are quite well integrated; but only under conditions of relative equitability for all. An ORSTOM report[9] notes that in countries of the South, "the poor remain incorporated within family and extra-family networks of social protection and mutual assistance, this incorporation produces integration and not exclusion." Unemployment and poverty, however, are significant risk factors for marginalization.

The marginalized person has been described by Park[10] as "one whom fate has condemned to live in two, not merely different but antagonistic cultures. . . ." The marginalized person attempts to gain release from a culture of domination to a culture of freedom; a situation of intense conflict

While different types of marginalization prevail, the focal point here will be on social marginalization where the occupational structure is the center of attention; social marginalization refers to a situation where a minority group is not allowed to participate fully in the institutions of the dominant society through prejudice and discrimination. This paper is part of a larger study on marginalization in different institutions in multiethnic societies.

Specifically, here, we examine the levels of participation of Indians and Africans in the administrative decision-making process. The level of participation in decision making is a useful indicator of the level of marginalization in a society. Our focus will be on the Public Sector, Education, State Boards, and Neighborhood Development Council (NDC) expenditures.

Results

Table 1.2: Senior Administrative Ranks by Ethnicity in the Public Service

Position	Total No.	# Indians (%)	# Africans (%)	# Others (%)
Ministers	19	13 (68)	3 (16)	3 (16)
Permanent Secretaries	15	9 (60)	6 (40)	0 (0)
PASs, Assts.	20	14 (70)	3 (15)	3 (15)
Accountant	104	22 (21)	68 (65)	14 (14)

(Heads)				
Senior Personnel Officers	13	0 (0)	13 (100)	0 (0)
Deputy PSs, Directors, and others	37	6 (16)	24 (65)	7 (19)

Source: Public Service Ministry Records, 2006

Indians are in large numbers in the upper echelons of the Ministry where they comprise 68 percent of the Ministers. At the level of the Permanent Secretary, both Indians and Africans are in fair equitable numbers. However, Africans control all other senior administrative and executive positions, such as, Deputy Permanent Secretaries, Principal Assistant Secretaries, Assistant Secretaries, Accountant Heads, and Senior Personnel Officers. Africans, therefore, are not marginalized in the upper levels of the hierarchy in the public service. There, however, is an evolving ethnic mix in the hierarchy of control.

Table 1.3: Ethnicity of Heads by Types of School

	Ethnicity			
	Indians %	Africans %	Others %	Total
Nursery	87(25)	177 (52)	78 (23)	342
Primary	149 (32)	225 (48)	91 (20)	465
Secondary	30 (24)	73 (57)	24 (19)	127
Total	266 (28)	475(51)	193(21)	934

Source: Ministry of Education, 2006

This Table illustrates the ethnicity of Heads in Nursery, Primary, and Secondary schools. Most Heads are Africans in all three types of school. Only in Primary schools do Indians show some competitiveness with Africans for Headships. Less than a third of school heads are Indians; and over half are Africans. Most school heads in Regions 2, 3, and 6 are Indians, while the majority of school heads in Regions 4, 5, and 10 are Africans.

Table 1.4:: Regional Education Officers

Ethnicity	2006 # (%)	2002 # (%)
Indians	5 (45)	4 (40)
Africans	6 (55)	5 (50)
Others	-	1 (10)
Total	11	10

Source: Teaching Service Commission, 2006

Under the PNC regime, it was not unusual to find on average 70% of African Regional Education Officers. Today, the ethnic imbalance has been narrowed to the point where we have 55% of African and 45% Indian (Regional Education Officers) REDOs.

Table 1.5: Deputy Heads by Ethnicity

Schools	Indians (%)	Africans (%)	Others (%)	Total
Nursery	-	1 (100)	-	1
Primary	49 (39)	50 (40)	26 (21)	125
Secondary	23 (26)	46 (53)	18 (21)	87
Total %	72 (34)	97 (46)	44 (20)	213

Source: Teaching Service Commission, June 15, 2006

About a third of Deputy Heads are Indians and nearly half are Africans for all three types of school. But almost equal numbers of Indians and Africans are Deputy Heads in Primary schools. Africans are two times more likely to occupy Deputy Headships than Indians. Interestingly, there is a growing number of 'Others' who occupy Deputy School Headships. About a third of Deputy Heads are Indians and just under half are Africans.

Table 1.6: University of Guyana Academic Staff by Ethnicity 2006

Faculty	# Indians %	# Africans %	# Others %	Total
Agriculture	0	5(71)	2(29)	7
Arts	0	1(100)	-	1
Education	9 (16)	41(75)	5(9)	55
Health	0	6(86)	1(14)	7
Faculty	# Indians %	# Africans %	# Others %	Total
Natural Sciences	20(44)	19(43)	6(13)	45
Social Sciences	9(20)	33(73)	3(7)	45
Technology	3(10)	22(76)	4(14)	29
Total	41 (22)	127 (67)	21 (11)	189

Source: University of Guyana, 2006

Table 5 shows a disproportionate number of African over Indian academic staff at the University of Guyana over recent years. African academics control the didactic dimension at faculty levels. The ethnic imbalance among academics is astounding - 22% of Indians as opposed to 67% of Africans occupy faculty positions. Only in Natural Sciences Indians are at par with Africans.

Table 1.7: Education State Boards by Ethnicity

Education State Boards	# Indians %	# Africans %	# Others %	# Total
U.G Council	11 (61)	6 (33)	1 (6)	18
National Library	4 (36)	7 (64)	0 (0)	11
C.P.C.E	4 (50)	4 (50)	0 (0)	8
G.T.I	2 (17)	8 (66)	2 (17)	12
President's College	5 (42)	6 (50)	1 (8)	12
Queen's College	3 (25)	7 (58)	2 (17)	12

Source: Office of the President Records, 2006

Both Indians and Africans have a fairly equitable distribution on the State Boards in Education. African numbers are relatively greater at the National Library, Government Technical Institute, and Queen's College. Indians enjoy some prominence on the University of Guyana Council, Cyril Potter College of Education; and with fair representation at President's College.

Table 1.8: Other State Boards by Ethnicity

State Boards	# Indian %	# African %	# Others %	Total
PAROLE	3 (25)	5 (41)	4 (12)	12
GPC	1 (50)	1 (50)	0 (0)	2
National commission on women	5 (45)	4 (36)	2 (18)	11
State Boards	**# Indian %**	**# African %**	**# Others %**	**Total**
Basic Needs Trust Fund	4 (40)	4 (40)	2 (20)	10
NICIL	2 (40)	2 (40)	1 (20)	5
GNCB	2 (100)	- (0)	- (0)	2
Iwokrama	1 (25)	- (0)	3 (75)	4
Guyana Water inc.	3 (30)	3 (30)	4 (40)	10
Wild Life Unit	2 (22)	7 (77)	- (0)	9
Wild Life Scientific	2 (40)	3 (60)	- (0)	5

Committee				
Poor Law Commission	3 (37)	4 (50)	1 (12)	8
Public Utilities Unit	2 (50)	2 (50)	- (0)	4
Tourism Authority	4 (40)	4 (40)	2 (20)	10
Bermine	- (0)	3 (100)	- (0)	3
Prerogative of Mercy	3 (50)	4 (50)	1 (12)	8

Source: Office of the President, 2006

Table 7 shows that in a review of 15 State Boards, an equitable distribution of ethnicity prevails. Indians outnumber Africans on only one Board, the National Commission on Women; Africans outnumber Indians on six Boards; and with Others outnumbering both Indians and Africans on one Board, Iwokrama. Interestingly, both major ethnic groups have equal Directorships on seven Boards.

The findings in a 'marginalization' study of 27 different State Boards in 2002 showed Africans were in the majority on 13 and Indians on 12, with two State Boards having equal numbers drawn from these two major ethnic groups.

The ethnic distribution of Directorships in that 2002 study today remains basically unchanged; and given the fact that the 2002 and 2006 studies used largely different State Boards, clearly, Africans then would have edged out the ethnic competition for Directorships on these Boards. A welcome development, however, is the evolving presence of minority Directors not from the two major ethnic groups.

Table 1.9: Projected Budgetary Allocations 2006 in Some African Areas in Region 4

Drainage and Irrigation	Beterverwagting Buxton Victoria Golden Grove Melanie Damishana Plaisisance Bladen Hall Ann's Grove Nabaclis	$15,043,180
Health	Beterverwagting Buxton Plaisance Nabaclis	$1,010,850
Agricultural Development	Buxton Melanie	$63,939,993

	Victoria Golden Grove Ann's Grove	

Source: GINA, 2006

Region Four is highlighted because it is (a) the most populated of all 10 Regions; (b) it has a significant African population; (c) it also houses Georgetown, the Capital City of Guyana and the seat of Central Government; (d) Georgetown has a large number of urban African dwellers; and (e) the PNCR controls this Region. Region 4 has a projected budgetary allocation of $128.6M for 2006. The Regional Administration has now assigned $89.5M in the areas of high African-concentration as indicated in Table 8. The residual sum of $39.1M has been allocated for projects in other parts of the Region.

These sample Tables are part of a larger study. But what do these Tables indicate? Clearly, that social marginalization among Africans is not significantly evidenced in the public sector.

Social marginalization where people are deprived of full participation in the society unquestionably is not a characteristic feature in the Guyana public sector. Today, with a greater ethnic mix in the public service, comparable socioeconomic status between Indians and Africans, and the evolving structures of political inclusiveness through the Dialog Joint Committees, Constitutional Amendments, Constitutional Commissions, and the role of the Opposition, the talk of social marginalization of Africans is totally absurd. Additional studies on marginalization, however, need to address areas of the private sector, too;

And marginalization may very well become a significant challenge in Caribbean integration; with the Caribbean Single Market and Economy (CSME) enabling free movement of labor and capital within CARICOM countries. Why a challenge? Many studies on marginalization in the labor market focus on the supply conditions of labor—education, work experience, ethnicity, demographic, family conditions, etc.; some studies now need to refocus on the demand for labor, i.e., job opportunities in areas where people reside. Clearly, different countries may have a different demand for labor, with different legislation, and different collective labor agreements, among other differences.

Notes

1. www.grad-inprowe.dk/summary.htm
2. Ibid.
3. Simmel, G. 1908. *Soziologie.* Leipzig: Duncker & Humblot. (*Sociology: Investigations on the Forms of Sociation*).
4. *Hintzen, P. Identity, nationalism and elite domination: The English-speaking West Indies.* In Ethnic Cleavage & Closure in the Caribbean Diaspora: Interactions of Race, Ethnicity, & Class, ed. *P. Misir.* Lanham, MD: University Press of America of the Rowman & Littlefield Group. (Forthcoming).

5. Ibid.
6. Frank, Andre Gunder. 1969. *Capitalism and underdevelopment in Latin America.* New York: Monthly Review Press.
7. Hintzen, op. cit.
8. Birbalsingh, F. 1997. *From Pillar to Post: The Indo-Caribbean Diaspora.* Toronto: Tsar Publications.
9. www.grad-inprowe.dk/summary.htm
10. Park, R. 1949. *Race and Culture.* New York: Free Press of Glencoe.

No Backsliding from Democracy

Evil forces constantly harangue anything that is good; all the good that comes out of the PPP/C Administration is spun as something bad; this is evil spin when good is presented as evil; anything evil sees everything as evil. But the PPP/C Government's good has always outmatched the reach of this evil. Evil forces have been hard at work from this Government's initiation in1992.

Today, dressed in the guise of respectability, these same forces present themselves as the people's representatives; twisting truth, not articulating the norms of objectivity and fundamental fairness.

These really are attacks on the people; onslaughts that sacrifice other citizens' rights and the public good to the pursuit of narrow political self-interests; a factionalism detrimental to democratic survival.

Vilifications include: Guyana is not free; Guyana is no democracy; Guyana has little economic development; Guyana marginalizes Africans; etc. Today, I want to address the first two and determine whether this spin can backslide Guyana's democracy to autocracy. Any exposition on freedom and democracy requires unearthing the PNC's legacy of repression.

Transition to democracy came in 1992 after 24 years of authoritarianism; when no institution made the government accountable to its people; an age of coercion where PNC rulers saw no limits to their authority and regulated all social life.

Distinguished Professor Clive Thomas in an interview in 2000 (interview by Dianne Feeley and David Finkel) described the PNC regime thus:

The truth however, is that this regime had been installed in power through a colonial maneuver with the electoral system before Independence in 1966, and maintained itself in power for nearly three decades through the systematic rigging of national elections and the employment of force and intimidation against all opposition to it.

During these 24 years, the National Security Act suspended the right to Habeas Corpus; and enabled the PNC regime to restrict and detain Guyanese without trial for an indefinite period. Part II of the National Security Act was reenacted in 1977 to indefinitely detain Guyanese without bail and trial. Some of today's broadcasters would not have survived the wrath of the Security law in those years!

The fact of the matter is that today, with no broadcasting law and little self-monitoring, media distortions are having a field day!

This is a paradox of freedom! Grand media distortions can happen amid the presence of fundamental human rights. The PPP/C Government reinstated human rights in this country; it has a historic track record since 1953 of promoting equality before the law for all persons; and making discrimination against all people unlawful through the Prevention of Discrimination Act 1997; and this Administration endorsed the Optional Protocol on the UN Covenant on Civil and Political Rights; the previous PNC regime was not a signatory.

In fact, the international-based Freedom House has deemed Guyana 'free' with regard to political rights and civil liberties since 1993. Guyana is free.

'Guyana is not a democracy' is another unproven onslaught on the integrity of this Administration. Let's explore this critique.

Democracy is more than casting ballots at election times. Karl (1990) refers to this as a 'fallacy of electoralism'. Goldstone et al (2005) in their study of transitions to and from democracy analyzed about 1,300 political, demographic, economic, social, and environmental variables for all countries globally with populations greater than 500,000 through 1955-2003.

They concluded that democracy has to do with 'election competitiveness' and 'inclusiveness'; and democracy can be measured through (1) and (2): (1) executive recruitment—how is the President elected and the frequency and competitiveness of elections? Note the limits on the President through Articles 90, 180, and 182 of the Guyana Constitution. The issue here is whether elections are free and have at least two parties contesting elections. Note that the 1992, 1997, and 2001 elections were free, fair, and transparent, and endorsed by international observers; note, too, the independent Guyana Elections Commission. (2) Competitiveness of political participation—the issue here is whether this Government limits political participation.

More countries today are less of a democracy not because of the quality of their elections, but more because of the quality of their political participation. Among other factors, absence of a Party from Parliament reduces quality participation.

Through 2001-2006, the PNC withdrew from Parliament as follows: March 25-December 5, 2002; March 28, 2003-April 14, 2003; March 19, 2004-August 5, 2004; and November 22-November 29, 2004. Almost two years of withdrawal delayed the processing and establishment of constitutional commissions and committee work in Parliament, negatively affecting the quality of PNC's political participation.

A sample of evolving political inclusiveness of the PNCR and other parliamentary parties is discerned through the following: (1) Jagdeo-Hoyte Joint Committees; (2) Constitutional Amendments creating: the Commissions; Parliamentary Standing Committee for constitutional reform; Parliamentary Sectoral Committees, (3) responsible opposition; and (4) membership on oversight committees and state boards. Government does not limit political participation.

Now what is the risk of Guyana's democracy backsliding to autocracy? Goldstone and others found that the risk is greater after 2 years, remaining until a democracy reaches age 15; though hardly backsliding after age 15. Only seven backslides in democracies aged over 15 occurred through 1955-2003: Brazil in 1964, Peru 1968, Philippines 1972, Chile 1973, Uruguay 1973, Fiji 1987, and Gambia 1994.

Goldstone and others argued that elections in young democracies are vulnerable to backsliding, especially to the second election; and that democracies in transition frequently have oppositions tottered by inadequate financing and mobilizational capacity.

They explained that elections force players to show whether they are willing to play with the new democratic rules. Democratic norms and practices are so strong today in Guyana that we are on the threshold of consolidation. But weak opposition elements, grounded in an undemocratic culture, may fear the new dispensation would disadvantage them in an electoral contest. Such opposition forces thrive under conditions of instability; and, therefore, a weakened democracy would present them with political opportunities; thus, some elements' acrimonious and threatening response to the new democratic culture; unsurprising, as an electoral contest is at hand.

The Truth about Democracy & Economic Development

There are different truths; truths engaging a different agenda of questions, to preserve the existing order of things, not the total truth; truths preserving a group's agenda to initiate change, another limited truth; both situations are people's perceptions of what their concept of truth is; both representing a biased version of the true reality. I present a few examples of limited truths; here goes:

Democracy has not taken hold in Guyana; economic development is still a far cry from being part of the woodwork in Guyana; the People's Progressive Party (PPP) is responsible for a lack of democracy and a lack of economic development through its failure to have constructed a national consensus immediately preceding the 1992 general elections.

Dr. David Hinds presented these sentiments and ideas in the Social and Economic Studies (54:1 2005, 67-82) of the University of the West Indies (UWI); and Hinds' complaint of the PPP bungling the opportunity to achieve a national consensus is based on a Working People's Alliance (WPA) version; an explanation lacking in completeness. Hinds neglected to inject the PPP's version into his discussion; and of course, to include, too, other versions pertinent to the discussion.

The PPP first initiated a proposal for the formation of a National Patriotic Front Government in 1977; not much happened then, except a few temporary alliances. A stronger arrangement emerged after the 1985 national elections when the Patriotic Coalition for Democracy (PCD) was established to remove the People's National Congress (PNC) dictatorship; bringing together five of the six opposition parties that contested the 1985 elections.

Eventually, a PCD program or platform was documented, but not publicly released. The PPP felt that it was mandatory to publicly disseminate such a program prior to the 1992 elections; enabling its access to all sections of society.

Disagreement emerged too on the choice of a Presidential candidate. The WPA initially agreed to have a person from one of the parties, but subsequently altered its position. The PPP consistently supported a person from one of the parties.

The PCD rejected the PPP's nominee Dr. Cheddi Jagan as the Presidential candidate because was an Indian; the PPP then suggested Dr. Roger Luncheon; he too was rejected because he was considered a communist.

Disagreement continued on party allocation for the joint slate for the National Assembly. The WPA suggested that half of the joint slate should be allocated equally to the four parties; the other half to the civic groups; under this formula, the PPP would have contributed only 12.5 % to the joint slate. Rejection of the proposal followed.

The PPP further suggested a provisional Presidential candidate and a provisional distribution for the joint slate in the proportion of 4-3-2-1, as one party had dropped out of the PCD; this proposal too was short-lived.

And so to which party could we attribute blame for not achieving a national consensus in 1992? Clearly, there was considerable disagreement within the PCD immediately preceding the 1992 national elections; and there may be other pieces of evidence on considerable disagreement within the PCD prior to 1992. Hinds' argument that the PPP bungled on the achievement of a national consensus, therefore, is difficult to accept.

In commenting on Guyana's fragile democracy and evolving economic development, why can we not simultaneously acknowledge the 'what is'? Maybe, Guyana is experiencing a democratization and economic development process not as fast-paced as we may wish; nonetheless, there are developments proceeding on both fronts, requiring some acknowledgement. Non-presentation of the 'what is' strengthens biases in any type of assessment. And there is no significant discussion of social indicators and social development in the Hind piece.

Indeed, the article in UWI's Social and Economic Studies contains no comparative data on economic development for the 1992-2005 period; suffice it to say that reasonable economic development has occurred and while it is not my intention here to assail this presentation with statistics, a few may point to some progressive development on the economic front; belying Hinds' assertion of a lack of economic development.

After 1992, Guyana was classified as a lower middle income country; carrying a Gross National Income (GNI) of US$649 million in 2000, US$682.1 million in 2003, and US$765.4 million in 2004; and the GNI per capita as US$860 in 2000, US$890 in 2003, and US$990 in 2004 compared to US$ 231 in 1991; minimum wage/salary: total increase was 615% from 1992 through 2001; $2801 (1992) and $20045 (2001).

During the period 2001-2004, the average annual real Gross Domestic Product (GDP) growth at factor cost was 1%, the average annual real GDP per capita was 0.7%; soaring inflation at 105% in 1991 is 7% today; interest rate hovering over 100% in 1992 has been cut to 13% today; and US$2 billion external debt at 1992 is now about US$1080 million; servicing of total debt now is a mere 10 % of exports of goods and on-factor services, reduced from 105% in 1992and 90% in 1993. Guyana's economic growth rate was 1.6% in 2004.

On September 9, 2005, Mr. Takatoshi Kato, Deputy Managing Director and Acting Chair of the Executive Board of the International Fund (IMF), said: "Guyana has made welcome progress under the PRGF arrangement. Despite the significant damage caused by the record floods in early 2005, program implementation has been broadly on track . . . macroeconomic stability has been maintained and inflation has remained low. Moreover, even in the face of sharply higher world oil prices, the overall balance of payments position continues to be in line with projections."

I think, too, that we need to consider the countervailing effects of the world economy on developing economies prior to making significant economic pronouncements. At any rate, whenever world development slows down, poor nations are disproportionately affected. The IMF (2003) reported that world development at US dollars and at current exchange rates declined from about 5.5% in 1970-80 to 2.3% in 1980-90 to 1.1% in 1990-2000. World income inequality rose since the 1970s. This trend is strongest when incomes are calculated at market-exchange-rate incomes (Wade, World Development, 2004).

In addition, consider the Sen Paradigm of development. Nobel Prize winning Economist Professor Amartya Sen has shown the futility of the traditional economic development perspectives of income, growth, and utility embracing GDP per capita, food security, and poverty. Sen believes that a better approach is to evaluate market outcomes and government actions in relation to valuable human results produced; a paradigm shift in development, moving away from income/growth/utility to a new beginning, a new focus on people's entitlements, capabilities, freedoms, and rights.

Note that the Human Development Index (HDI) is largely sourced from Sen's work. Note, too, the three critical human capabilities in the HDI—literacy rate, income, and life expectancy at birth; a mixed bag of social and economic indicators. The Sen Paradigm refutes the significance of a total focus on economic development, perhaps to the detriment of social development; significantly applying social indicators now becoming the norm of developing economies as a response to HDI.

The following key indicators of health have progressively improved over recent years: infant mortality, maternal mortality, doctor/patient ratio, nurse/patient ratio, and bed/patient ratio. Today, the national enrolment ratios for both primary and secondary schools are increasingly better than a decade ago; but hinterland Regions still hovering around a third in secondary school enrolment. By 2002, 74.2 of the people had access to safe drinking water; excepting Region 8 where only 26.6% had access. Electrification is now within the reach of 75% of households.

Hinds asserts that the democratization process in Guyana is inadequate. In a democracy, a citizen is expected to appreciate diversity; actively participate in the society; be well informed; and support the state. There absolutely is no disagreement that democracy involves more than casting the ballot at election times.

Faced with the legacy of an authoritarian regime, the new Government faced enormous problems in establishing a democracy because of some persisting autocratic traditions, beliefs, and values unsuited to a functioning democracy. Notwithstanding such adversities, Freedom House, a highly-respected international group, depicts Guyana as free and high on political rights and civil liberties in 2005 as it has done since 1993.

Has Guyana not made some strides in the reconstruction of democracy? Do we not see social developments in this country? I would answer in the affirmative. But we must do more in the cause of development; projecting limited truths may be unhelpful. And this projection may very well not be Dr. Hinds' intent.

Perhaps, the Editor of Social and Economic Studies can commission a contribution on social and economic development in post-1992 Guyana.

Promises, Promises

There are promises and promises; true and false promises. Some see the PPP/C's promises as suspect and others as authentic. The PPP/C's promises are authentic; how so? I believe the answer to this question requires a prior question: what has the PPP/C Government done over the last 14 years?

I am not suggesting that other contesting parties' promises are not authentic; the Guyanese people will be the judge on the authenticity of their promises. But most of the other parties saving the PNCR1G have no record on which the masses can apportion judgment; whereas the PPP/C has accomplishments, significant accomplishments.

Those who cast aspersions on the ruling party's promises imply that these promises should have been fulfilled within the last 14 years. Accomplishments modernizing the face of Guyana and the magnitude of their impact during this period would clearly demonstrate how limited time and space were available for other productive engagements. Examples of some of these PPP/C's achievements may suffice to showcase the enormity of progress; and progress is relative, not absolute, a scenario where there indeed would be some unfinished business.

Table 1.11 depicts the economy as positive which generally gets lost in the scramble to demonstrate negatives. The modest inflation and interest rates, and the constant exchange rate are the pillars of Guyana's macroeconomic stability.

Since 1992, there has been a 625% tax free allowance and an 886% increase in the minimum wage to facilitate an enhanced purchasing power.

Table 1.10: Economic Indicators

	2006	*2005*	*2004*	*2003*	*1992*	*1991*
Inflation rate	3.4%	8.3%	5.5%	4.9%	-	90%
Per capita income		US$900	-	-	-	US$231
Minimum wage/salary		$24,828 (US$124)	-	-	$2801 (US$22)	-
Average lending rate	16.45%	15.24%	15.65%	15.71%	>30%	-
Tax-free allowance	$300,000 (US$1,500)	-	-	-	$48,000 (US$380)	-

Sources: Ministry of Finance; Bank of Guyana

The annual exports of Guyana's major commodities—sugar, rice, dried bauxite, molasses, and timber/plywood — have increased in volume.

Table 1.11: Export Performance

Sugar: (tonnes)	2005	1991
	231,700	157,000
Rice: (tonnes)	2005	1991
	182,200	50,000
Dried Bauxite: (tonnes)	2000	1991
	2,421,000	975,000
Molasses: (kg)	2000	1991
	39,776	955
Timber/plywood: (cubic metres)	2000	1991
	184	16

Source: Bureau of Statistics

Table1. 12: Education Budget & %age CXC Passes

YEAR	%age BUDGET	CXC PASSES (Grades 1-4)
2005	13.7	79.1
2002	14	77.1
1992	6.01	47.52

Source: NCERD

Table 2.3 shows that as the education budget increases, the CXC success rate increases; and this Government continues to pump enormous sums into education annually because it understands the relationship between education and national development. General secondary enrolment was 35% in 1992; today, it stands at 69%; and in the 1992/2005 period, 84 schools were built—21 Secondary; 24 Primary; and 39 Nursery.

I do not want to emblazon this piece with an entire trail of statistics. Perhaps, it would be useful for voters to refer to government information on development matters, and then go out and verify them for themselves; and I am convinced, that having executed this exercise, confused voters will see the light of day; new witnesses to the enormity of national development over the last 14 years.

But there also have been a few downturn cycles in the economy over the last decade; among other factors, the downturn impact came through the senseless post-elections violence that emerges at each election in Guyana; the economic stranglehold that the World Trade Organization has on poor developing countries; only reaching financial viability after about 10 years in office, given the external debt of US$2.1 billion and an inheritance of practical financial bankruptcy in 1992; the Great Flood of 2005; and the world economic situation.

The world economy currently is in bad shape; emasculating developing countries. Under-Secretary-General for Economic and Social Affairs of the United Nations Social and Economic Council Jose Antonio Ocampo recently launched the report "World Economic Situation and Prospects 2006."

Ocampo asserted that the world economy experienced an economic slow down since 2004: global investment anemia disrupting global economic growth rate, creating a disorderly adjustment of macroeconomic imbalances; higher oil prices of about $60 per barrel; the crash of house prices, especially in the U.S. negatively impacting global consumption and demand; high unemployment growth; and many developing countries' experience of structural unemployment and underemployment impacting poverty reduction.

While statistical data do not always translate into human development, there has to be some agreement that the economic scene has considerably improved from what the baseline data suggest in 1992; economic and social enhancement has happened.

Perhaps, if those new PPP/C's promises that some people thought should have been fulfilled over the last decade were really satisfied, then what would have happened to the current enormity of progress? Could it not be that the working class people of this country savor this current spate of development? Let us be patient; the new PPP/C's promises will find a place on the production line in the next few weeks as a new PPP/C Administration takes office.

Toward Reducing Over-Politicization

The scramble for power is an ugly sight in Guyana. Everything else takes second place in this insufferable 'power' stampede; creating in its scurrilous path a charade of unscrupulous demands. Consider these: the tiresome and unnecessary calls for house-to-house verification when reasonable sanitation procedures are in place; the unbearable demands for shared governance when the politics of inclusivity already have begun in earnest. A charade of structured unscrupulous demands may contribute to the construction of over-politicization.

Anyway, we tend to understand these demands through isolating and examining them, as if they were really the beginning and the end, and as if they are the result of something immediately preceding them, as if they have no relation to anything from the distant past, as if they are acting in solo. But these demands are a link in a chain, caused by similar occurrences from the past; earlier occurrences created through the wills, urges, and desires of several opinion leaders; these wills, urges, and desires are the forces that produce new demands. However, the present and past demands are all connected. Consider the following annotations from 1997 to highlight this connection:

1. The 'kith and kin' politics, referring to African ethnicity, was used by the PNC/R Leader at the 1997 election.
2. Hoyte, when presenting his demands in March 2001 said: "It is therefore the considered view of the leadership of the People's National Congress Reform that business as usual is neither reasonable nor possible at this time." Hoyte's demands were issued against a background of PNC/R protests and violence unleashed by the dogs of war. This remark was quite consistent with other oppositional annotations contributing to instability in the society.
3. The statement by the PNC/R of making the country 'ungovernable'.
4. A former senior PNCR Central Executive member remarked that it "is in the business of trying to get the government of the day out of office. There is nothing wrong with any statements which say that as an opposition party, we are attempting to remove the government."
5. Jerome Khan, a PNCR Member of Parliament, cited the case of a senior ranking person of the PNCR, as suggesting that attacks against Indians will produce positive outcomes.
6. Use of the 'slow fire, more fire' phrase by the PNCR during the last election campaign.
7. Evidence of a PNCR electoral candidate for the 2001 election inciting violence.

These sustained inflammatory circumstances and annotations historically have been the framework through which politicians issue excessive and unreasonable demands; at any rate, the end-results are instability and over-politicization. Under these conditions, political trickery and intrigue replace idealism and fear and selfishness take the place of disinterested courage, so says Nehru.

Too much wasted time is spent on personalized and naïve politicking, to the detriment of addressing serious social issues; the media houses partner this naïve politicking. The media sustain a political scorecard that feeds on insular content. The Guyanese media, arguably, may have failed the people of this country through their informational, communicational, and educational incapacity to consistently disseminate and discuss objectively and with fundamental fairness what matters in this country. Editors and owners of the media may need to reassess their existing over-politicized orientations and their over-zealous political partnerships; and consider a generic approach to addressing issues. The society now has become over-politicized; and this is an evil.

Against this backdrop of over-politicization, some politicians and media operatives carry on this charade as if the people of this country are not knowledgeable and capable; everything is reduced to politicking and ruse. They use an unsavory 'quantum leap' tool to draw non-evidentiary conclusions to sustain their distortions. These charades, taking the form of unscrupulous 'demands', demoralize and over-politicize the society. Let us remember that one of the goals of over-politicization is to destroy human free will.

As people may seemingly become captives to these outlandish demands, are we saying that these people have no choice over their own behavior, or are their actions only shaped by these infectious tirades that today fill the political and broadcasting landscape of this country? The fact that these political and media distortions do push people to some action that they may not have contemplated, is powerful evidence that the warped discourses on ruthless demands do not have the effect they claim to have.

People's behavior determines not only what they become as individuals, but the roles they can play in changing society. What we need to understand is that most people develop an identity in society; but it does not mean that each person becomes some mirror image of some force in society. Both society and the individual change; but how they change also depends on the choices each person makes.

If people merely comply with this over-politicized model of society, then political trickery and intrigue will win the day. Fortunately, human behavior is not shaped to merely acquiesce; human behavior has the capacity to oppose dubious limitations imposed by broadcasting and political charlatans. Many people, as social beings, fortunately, can redefine the terms of their existence through the choices they make in negotiating this over-politicized conception of this country.

People can change this over-politicization in Guyana; people have to examine any unscrupulous demand, asking the following questions, among others, 'are these demands good for this country?' 'Who are the chief beneficiaries of these demands?' 'Are these demands birthed in selfishness?' 'What is lurking behind these demands?' A dispassionate search for truthfulness in the answers will dissipate over-politicization; a necessity in this election season.

Scrutinize Hoyte's Abysmal Record

"The world is what it is; men who are nothing, who allow themselves to become nothing, have no place in it" (Naipaul). I don't want to be as hard as Naipaul in describing some politicians as 'nothing'. But political leaders through their administrations have to be evaluated as to whether their outcomes over the years are negative or amount to nothing. Promises made by politicians are useful, but they also can be broken. So voters need information on politicians' record, in order to make an informed choice and judgment on March 19. The record largely will determine the veracity and credibility of promises. Keep in mind the new label for the main minority party—PNC/Reform, and the slogan 'Putting Guyana First'. Other parties and their slogans are relevant here, too.

In effect, if we are evaluating the Leader of the PNC Reform, Mr. Hugh Desmond Hoyte's political credentials, then he must be judged on his record. The PNC is touting Hoyte's experience as the winning factor on March 19. Therefore, we must review his track record as President of Guyana that runs the gamut from 1985 through 1992.

We shall review some of the Order Papers of the National Assembly between 1985 through 1992. Incidentally, some of these documents are missing for those years when the PNC extended their life in the National Assembly several times. Here goes.

In Notice Paper #16, published on March 6, 1986, a motion was presented by Reepu Daman Persaud for the National Assembly (NA) to hold local government elections immediately after a reconstituted elections commission was established, a new voters' list prepared, and a Commonwealth or CARICOM observers' team decided upon. The PNC, the majority in the NA threw it out. Note that this was a period filled with rigged elections from 1968, and the fact that local government elections were long overdue. In fact, under PNC rule, local government elections were first held in April 1970, and sixteen years later, there still was no local government election. The PPP/C Administration held local government elections in August 1994, and another one is due shortly after the impending national election.

Another Notice Paper of the same date was presented. This was a motion by Janet Jagan, calling on the NA to recommend that adequate medical personnel be made available in all rural and hinterland districts, and that all health centers be adequately staffed, given enough drugs, medical supplies, and means of communication. This motion was not approved by the PNC-dominated NA, demonstrating PNC's low priority assigned to Hinterland Guyana.

Janet Jagan moved another motion, which was published on March 16, 1986. This motion alluded to the shortage of milk, either locally-produced, or imported, to satisfy the children and adults' needs. In her motion, she called on the PNC Government to ensure that sufficient supplies of milk became available through importation and be equitably distributed to all of Guyana's children. Again, during Hoyte's Presidency, this proposal was rejected. This was a period in which the incidence of malnutrition and infant mortality rate was high among children. Today, Guyana can boast of a mere 15% of infants with low birth weight. Infant mortality rate in the Hoyte era was almost double what it is today; now it is 56 per 1,000, still high, but it has considerably declined.

PPP Parliamentarian Reepu Daman Persaud moved a motion to address charges of discrimination sweeping through the PNC Administration. This motion called on the NA to appoint a Parliamentary Commission, inclusive of TUC representatives, to investigate all charges of discrimination in the PNC Administration and its Agencies, and to present reports to the NA. The motion was not accepted. It was not until 1997 in a PPP/C Administration that an effort was effected to establish the Integrity Commission. Subsequently, through an Amendment to the Constitution, the Ethnic Relations Commission now will become a reality to speak to racial discriminatory charges across all institutions. Previously, the PPP/C attempted to establish a race relations commission and submitted the name of Bishop Randolph George as its head. But Hoyte rejected the Bishop. Last year, the NA approved the establishment of an Ethnic Relations Commission. The PNC's position under Hoyte's tutelage, therefore, seemed to apportion low priority to discriminatory matters, a line quite consistent with their 1986 decision to reject Reepu Daman Persaud's motion.

Eusi Kwayana tackled the right of dismissed workers to be heard through a motion to the NA in 1986. Kwayana argued that no civilian or other personnel of the Government, or of the public sector, should be dismissed or be imposed with a final penalty without the right to be heard and the right of defense against specific charges, and that where a judicial body rules in favor of the worker, reinstatement should ensue. Again, this motion did not find favor with the PNC Parliamentarians. It is useful to note that major labor legislation reforms, addressing the rights of the worker, inter alia, were introduced in the PPP/C Administration. One of these was the Termination of Employment and Severance Pay Act 1997 which addressed workers' rights.

The allegation of corruption, which apparently is in vogue today, first touched the NA in 1986. A motion moved by Kwayana, called on the PNC Government to introduce integrity legislation, impacting senior Government officials, members of the Government, and all Parliamentarians. The NA rejected this motion. In fact, the Integrity Commission Act was passed in 1997 under a PPP/C Administration, making provisions for setting up the Integrity Commission, and to secure integrity of personnel in public life.

S.F. Mohamed called on the PNC Government to institute a school feeding program that would include a daily supply of milk to all children in kindergartens and other children nationwide. The proposal was rejected. The school feeding program over the Burnham/Hoyte era was funded through a Memorandum of Understanding between the Government and the Food and Agriculture Organization (FAO). The feeding program had a very checkered life during the 1968/1992 period where the school-feeding program was available only at some points. In 1996, the PPP/C Administration made a landmark decision to locally fund a comprehensive school-feeding program. Keep in mind that prior to 1996; the school feeding program was internationally funded.

Haripersaud Nokta called on the NA in 1986 to abolish road tolls because they constituted a burden on overtaxed Guyanese, and resulted in costly collections. Needless to say that the proposal was not accepted.

The Economic Recovery Program (ERP) in 1989 was not Hoyte's brainchild. The ERP was instituted and driven by the World Bank and the International Monetary Fund (IMF), which radically reduced the Government's role in the economy. At that time, the country was economically bankrupt, as attested to by Finance Minister Carl Greenidge.

Since the early 1980s, the bauxite industry was a net user of foreign exchange coupled with high production costs. In 1988, rice production was 130,000 metric tons, with 150,000 tons in 1991, and 168,000 tons in 1992.Inadequate foreign exchange for chemicals and other needs, and low prices paid to rice farmers produced a crisis in the rice industry in 1988. Compare this situation with 1999 when rice production reached 365,000 tons. When the PPP/C took office in 1992, sugar was imported from Guatemala. In 1989, 167,000 tons of sugar were produced. Sugar tonnage reached 321,000 in 1999.

Hoyte's record shows a pattern, a pattern of sustaining vested self-interests as opposed to the people's interests. His abysmal record amounted to almost nothing until his regime was rescued first, by the World Bank and IMF, and second, by the PPP/C in 1992.

Hoyte's tutelage showed that he held no local government election, gave low priority to medical service in the Hinterland, sustained low health status among children, apportioned minimum concern for discriminatory matters, mocked around with workers' rights, showed no interest in an integrity commission, and displayed no apprehension for a checkered school feeding program. This partial list of Hoyte's record, demonstrating not much concern for people's interests, amounts 'nothing' in politics. Voters have a duty to scrutinize Hoyte's appalling record and make an informed choice on March 19.

EMBRACING INSULAR POLITICS THROUGH A 17-POINT PLAN

Hoyte's 17-point plan issued in March last year has become the new poster boy manifesto of the People's National Congress/Reform (PNC/R) Party, and has largely replaced the Agenda 21 inclusion as well as other aspects of its Manifesto in 2001. Or at least, the electoral passion for Agenda 21 seems to have suddenly dissipated. From the onset, we need to say that this plan is not really a plan, but a laundry list of demands. Several of these demands are generic and can be applied in almost any nation building programs. However, the People's Progressive Party/Civic (PPP/C) already had many aspects of this generic plan enshrined in its Manifesto 2001, long before these demands were presented by Hoyte last year. So the generic aspects of the plan are not unique to the PNC/R.

Creating Instability

Hoyte's demands were issued against a background of PNC/R protests and violence unleashed by the dogs of war. In that climate, in March 2001, Hoyte said in a speech to the nation when the demands were presented, "It is therefore the considered view of the leadership of the People's National Congress Reform that business as usual is neither reasonable nor possible at this time." This remark and some nefarious activities are quite consistent with other PNC/R's annotations contributing to instability in the society. Here are a few:

1) The statement by the PNC/R of making the country ungovernable still is being utilized.
2) A senior PNC/R Central Executive member said that it "is in the business of trying to get the government of the day out of office. There is nothing wrong with any statements which say that as an opposition party, we are attempting to remove the government."
3) The 'kith and kin' politics, referring to African ethnicity, was used by the PNC/R Leader at the 1997 election.
4) Jerome Khan, a PNC/R Member of Parliament, cited the case of a senior ranking person of the PNC/R, as suggesting that attacks against East Indians will produce positive outcomes.
5) Use of the 'slow fire, more fire' phrase by the PNC/R during the last election campaign.
6) There is evidence of a PNC/R electoral candidate for the 2001 election inciting violence.

These inflammatory circumstances as concocted ingredients making for political instability are not characteristic of the functions of a responsible opposition. How can you ask for implementing demands for national development when at the same time you are creating 'instability' scenarios? While many of Hoyte's demands, largely, were addressed through the Jagdeo/Hoyte Dialog which created six Joint Committees, it is instructive to note that Hoyte's demands, intrinsically, already part of the PPP/C Government's existing program prior to the 2001 election, would have become a reality anyway without the Dialog.

The 17 Demands

Here in a nutshell are the 17 demands: resuscitation of the bauxite industry; immediate enquiry to police brutality; immediate termination of on the monopoly of the radio, and introduce independent management of GTV, GBC, and the Guyana Chronicle; reviving depressed communities; create job-relief programs; end to discrimination on housing and land distribution; providing basic infrastructures for disadvantaged communities; bring an end to the politicization of the public service; introduce local government reform; implement check-off for the PSU; provide guaranteed subventions to Critchlow Labor College; national consensus needed on border and security issues; recapitalization of the GDF a must; introduce tendering and contracting reforms; end all corruption; introduce all-party management of parliamentary affairs; and put into operation all constitutional reforms. I will now review these demands where quite a few overlap with each other. Technically, then, the demands number less than 17.

Resuscitation of the Bauxite Industry

One of Hoyte's 17 demands had to do with the resuscitation of the bauxite industry. Exports for mining and quarrying rose from $5.2B in 1991 to $13.9B in 1999. Over the last 10 years, the PPP/C Government provided in excess of US$5M annually to the Linden bauxite operations. The PPP/C Government, prior to the 2001 election, indicated that it will reevaluate lower grade aluminous laterites that were rejected before as a feed source to regional alumina operations, and will aid the exploration of smaller close-to-the-surface deposits by the locals. Efforts, therefore, to resuscitate the bauxite industry and the Linden community started since 1993, and therefore, well before Hoyte made this demand last year.

Bermine now has been privatized through the President's intervention. Government made available $212M to cover the cost of severance and training. Bermine pays no utility bills, as Government picks up these expenses. With Linmine, Government brokered an agreement with the relevant Unions for the issuance of a 'separation package'. Region 10 where Linden and Linmine are located, received $219.7M in 2002 to increase the provision of social services. Through Linden Economic Advancement Program (LEAP), 12.5M Euro Dollars are now available to developing the Linden community. At this time, about 50 business proposals have been submitted for funding under LEAP.

Ending State Monopoly of the Media

Another of Hoyte's demand had to do with ending the political monopoly of state radio, GTV, GBC, and the Guyana Chronicle. Long before Hoyte spoke about terminating state monopoly of the media, many committees and draft reports were completed in the 1990s, including a Seminar at Hotel Tower in 2000, all focusing on the establishment of a broadcasting authority. While there still is no broadcasting authority, we need to understand that these apriority efforts were part of a significant process to reach that goal. A Joint Committee on Radio Monopoly, Non-Partisan Boards and Broadcasting Legislation was set up last year. Interestingly, some of the earlier documents, indeed, did lay the basis for some discussions in the Joint Committee and a few were even appendicized in the Joint Committee's report. The Joint Committee's report was sent to the Attorney General's Chambers for legal drafting in preparation for Parliament.

Depressed Communities and Infrastructures

Another of Hoyte's demand had to do with meeting the needs of depressed communities. In 1992, about 86% of the people were living below the poverty line. Today, it is about 35%. This poverty reduction happened over the last eight years, and not a year ago since Hoyte made his demands. Poverty is unevenly distributed in this country, and so poverty reduction programs, initially, will have to touch areas with the highest incidence of poverty, such as, the hinterland and the rural coastal areas. These areas have the highest poverty gap, with the hinterland at 44.9 and rural coastal at 11.3 in 1999. The Dialog subsequently this year designated Non Pariel/Enterprise, De Kinderen, Meten-Meer-Zorg and Buxton as depressed communities. A total of $60M was allocated for electricity, drainage and roads for these areas. But other communities, indeed, with high poverty incidence, will shortly be addressed.

This year's Budget has allocated about $2B on projects to enhance standard of living of the poor and others. These projects are now being administered through (SIMAP0, Basic Needs Trust Fund (BNTF), LEAP, the Poverty Fund, and the Poor Rural Communities Project.

During the PNC ruling era, budget allocations to many African villages were minimal. Today, every sector and community are touched by the PPP/C budget. With respect to the three historic African villages, Victoria, Hopetown, and Buxton, for this year, a total of about $45M was spent on infrastructures. Buxton alone incurred infrastructural costs to the tune of $44.3M this year so far.

Other infrastructural works include rehabilitating Mahaica/Rosignol Road and constructing 59 bridges between Timehri and Rosignol. Preliminary works to rehabilitate 9 additional bridges and 53 culverts have commenced. This year, $700M was provided to construct a number of farms to market roads. Other works have begun on many roads including Sisters Village, La Retraite, Section "B" Sophia, New Forest, Mon Repos, Kwebanna/Kumaka, Port Kaituma, Golden Fleece, Cotton Field/Aurora, Riverstown, Dartmouth, Goed Intent, Hogg Island, De Amstel, Bare Root, Jonestown, Haslington, Kuru Kuru, Blairmont, Zorg en Hoop, Litchfield, Woodley Park, Ithaca, Letter Kenney/Auchline, Orealla/Siparuta.

Job Training

Job training programs for youth are available, again before Hoyte made his demands last year. At Mid-2002, a sum of $18.4B, provided by the Education, Health, Housing and Water, and Culture, Youth and Sport Ministries, was allocated for youth development in the President's Youth Choice Initiative program. The Ministry of Culture, Youth and Sport, on its own, currently utilizes $.5B for youth training. Some of the youth programs aimed at providing job skills and administered under the Ministry of Culture, Youth and Sport and the Office of the President are: Youth Entrepreneurial Skills Program, The Opportunity Corp., The Angoy Drop-In Center, The President's Youth Choice Initiative, The President's Youth Award Republic of Guyana Program, and The Commonwealth youth Program. Further, the Private Sector projected that in 2002 about $103M as investment in 67 projects, will generate 3,500 new jobs.

Recapitalizing the Joint Security Forces

The Guyana Defense Force (GDF) has not been neglected, as suggested by Hoyte in one of his 17 demands. We need to note that the recapitalization of the

GDF started way back in 1993.For example, in 1990, the GDF's total budget was a mere G$185.5M, and in 2000, the GDF obtained G$2,396.30B.The Guyana Police Force (GPF) in 2002 received a capital budget of $470.5M and a current budget of $2.5B.The GPF has come a long way from the pittance doled out to it in 1991.Clearly, there was tremendous recapitalization happening in the Joint Security Forces long before Hoyte's demands last year, and, indeed, this recapitalization is continuous.

Housing Discrimination

Hoyte's other demand made last year pertained to discrimination in housing. Since, 1992, over 50,000 house lots were distributed. The major ethnic groups have received fundamentally fair proportions on the basis of their respective demographics, as evidenced by the Housing statistics. 91 housing schemes and 65 of the 120 squatter settlements have now been regularized. Also, there is a strategic plan to issue about 7,000 land titles per year. People must not forget that the Ministry of Housing was abolished during the Hoyte regime. Early this year, the Minister presented in March 2002 a White Paper in Parliament, addressing national land distribution policy. The PNC/R needs to debate the issues in this White Paper in Parliament, not in the media outlets.

Local Government Reform

Local government neglect was a characteristic feature during the PNC's ruling years. Hoyte has demanded local government reform, but did nothing about it in his years in office. Prior to 1994, the last local government election was held in 1970. Local government election was administered in 1994, and the next election possibly will be held in 2003. Annual subventions are given to local government bodies, and the Amerindian development Fund now is at $310M. The Urban Development Program, initiated in 2000, and comprising US$25M, is currently being implemented to upgrade the towns. The PPP/C Manifesto 2001 stipulated that that the Local Government Act, Chapter 28:02 will be amended to give greater autonomy to Neighborhood Democratic Councils. Also, earmarked for revision in the Manifesto 2001 is the Municipal and District Councils Act, Chapter 28:01, which will give autonomy to municipal councils.

A Joint Committee on Local Government Reform was established through the Dialog. This Committee's findings and recommendations are still being compiled. However, the Committee's term of office expired in May 2002, and an extension of three months is being sought from President Jagdeo and Mr. Hoyte to complete the Report. At this time, consideration of an extension will not happen as Hoyte has placed the Dialog on pause.

Constitutional Amendments

Hoyte in his demands asked for the implementation of constitutional reforms. But his party's absence from Parliament has impeded the Amendment's form and content in reality. A number of constitutional amendments, showing the emergent structures for inclusiveness, were passed. Some of these were as follows:

- The Constitution (Amendment) (No.2) Act 200.This Amendment created five (5) Constitutional Commissions. These Commissions represent another component making for inclusiveness. They are the Ethnic relations Commission, Indigenous People's Commission, Commission for the Rights of the Child, Commission for Human Rights, and Women and Gender Equality Commission.
- The Constitution (Amendment) (No. 6) Act 2001.The Constitution was amended at Article 119A.The amendment provides for the establishment of a Parliamentary Standing Committee for Constitutional Reform, aimed at frequently reviewing the efficacy of the functioning of the Constitution. All members of Parliament are eligible for membership.
- The Constitution was amended at Article 119B.This Amendment provides for the establishment of parliamentary sectoral committees providing oversight to Government policy and administration, including: natural resources; economic services; foreign relations; and social services. Again, all Parties in Parliament are eligible for membership.
- The Constitution (Amendment) (No. 4) Act 2001.This Amendment repealed and reenacted Article 13 of the Constitution. The Amendment provides for the political system of the state to set up an inclusionary democracy, enabling citizen participation. The recently-concluded CARICOM Heads of Government Meeting in Guyana initiated civil society participation for the first time in such conferences. President Jagdeo, the new Chairman of CARICOM for the next six months, enabled one day to be set aside for the theme, 'Encounter with Civil Society'.
- The Constitution (Amendment) (No. 2) Act 2001.Article 71 of the Constitution was altered to enable local government to engage many people in governance.
- Article 78B was inserted in the Constitution. The electoral system below the Regional Democratic Councils provides for the participation, representation, and accountability of individuals and voluntary groups to the voters. These individuals and groups are in addition to the political parties.

All these constitutional amendments help to expand the structures of inclusiveness, albeit that a few are now becoming operational. Parliament will have to initiate discussions on these Amendments to give meaning and life to their applications. The PNC/R's absence from Parliament retards the social growth of the Amendments.

Reforming the Tendering and Contracting Procedures

Again, Hoyte has asked for reforms to the tendering procedures. The Constitution requires the Auditor General to annually submit reports of public accounts to Parliament requirement was not met for about 10 years prior to 1992 since 1992, audited annual reports of public accounts have been submitted to Parliament. The Central Tender Board Secretariat was installed, with public consultations held with contractors and consultants to improve the tendering and procurement mechanism. The Government subsequently applied several measures, as, public opening of tenders, examining and auditing the tender process by the Office of the Auditor General, nominating independent evaluators, presenting written evaluations, and scheduling frequent meetings of the tender boards. Clearly' a number of reforms to the tendering practices has occurred prior to Hoyte's demands made last year.

Insular Politics

We need to understand that this Administration is still working through its term in office, and at this time, is under two years old. The PPP/C Administration still has considerable tasks to complete, tasks that are embellished in its Party Manifesto 2001. Hoyte made his demands through his 17-point plan to construct a perception for his supporters to believe that he still commanded the reigns of leadership in his party and still can drive the nation-building process through his own image of statesmanship. However, Hoyte was enabled this opportunity to renew and reaffirm his statesmanship through the Dialog. Indeed, he squandered this significant occasion to rise above the fray of partisan and insular politics to reach and embrace the acme of nationalism. The insularity is exposed through the demands purporting to provide maximum benefits only to PNC/R supporters and to attract crass populism.

At any rate, several of Hoyte's demands made last year were not novel, as they already were incorporated into the PPP/C Administration's program well before 2001 election and well before Hoyte told the nation of his so-called ground-breaking plan. In any case, the PPP/C Government is moving apace to fulfill its mandate of nation building, amid the tactics of an irresponsible opposition.

Political Bias not Good for Crime Fighting

Finger-pointing on the crime situation goes on ad nauseum in Guyana; "the Government is unable to curb crime" has become the unholy mantra for weakened opposition elements as the election season advances. And then there are those who aspire to have an explanation for everything, including crime; but their postulates are unwholesome; Why? These people's behavior to crime solving is more akin to the behavior of an attack dog against the Government; clearly, no appreciation and focus on the fundamentals of crime solving; their crime-solving approach has an obsessive marital relationship with political posturing; their talk on crime-solving has nothing to do with crime; only cheap political points; power fixation; amid a labyrinth of 'crime' victims.

The Cabinet is not the professional crime-fighting force in this country; the Guyana Police Force (GPF) as is the case with police forces globally is assigned the right to protect the citizenry; GPF is the crime-fighting force. Today, the GPF is better equipped than ever since its beginnings in 1838. GPF also did have a special crime unit to tackle abnormalities in crime; this special unit as the crime-fighting force against 'kick-down-the-door' crime wave in the 1980s was pretty much the same unit deployed in the crime wave in 2002-2003; but this unit was not too long ago disbanded as a result of the oppositional elements' public outcry. Incidentally, public discourses on the need for a new special crime unit have now reentered the talk shop; and there is a consistent view that a special crime unit may be the answer to the sporadic crime wave. Why then did the opposition elements call for the special unit's death?

On another front, the GPF is a colonial product; and these are not colonial times; and with the current raging security challenges, makeover in police behavior is fast becoming the in-thing; new strategies will have to replace the GPF traditional modus operandi. And, indeed, structure must follow strategy. In this regard, President Jagdeo has enlisted support from a former New York top cop Bernard Kerik to assist with the GPF restructuring and security reform. Of course, there are the usual suspects pouring 'cold water' on any new proposal; organizational blockers, people who contract a disease when they see progress. This time their beef is: Why the PPP/C Government did not restructure the GPF before now?

Through the PPP/C 1992-2006 tenure, these blockers may very well not root for, and would ask the following questions on prioritized programs and projects, now completed: Why build 84 schools? Why immunize 95% of one-year olds against tuberculosis? Why immunize 89% of one-year olds against measles? Why increase secondary school enrolment from 35% in 1991 to 72% in 2006? Why address the abysmal state of CXC passes in 1992 when it was only 47% to reach 79% in 2005? Why construct new hospitals at Linden and Lethem? Why build a new hospital in New Amsterdam in 2005? Why have diagnostic centers at Port Mourant, Diamond, and Mahaicony? Why have 63 sites nationally to advance the Prevention of Mother-to-Child Transmission? Why create a 600-strong neighborhood Police Unit? Why allocate 70,000 house lots? Why create 100 housing schemes? Why regularize 120 squatter settlements? Why install 1,000 miles of pipeline from Charity through Crabwood Creek? Why install 150 drilled water wells and hand-dug wells in Regions 1, 2, and 8? Why give titles and demarcation to 50 Amerindian communities? And this is not an exhaustive list of completed projects.

Clearly, in any governmental tenure, some things will be left out and would be part of the production line in the next administration. And no one will disagree that the time has come for Security reform; only now, why? In Guyana's recent history from the 1980s, the GPF special crime unit's general effectiveness against crime abnormalities may have induced a staying of the hand on security reform, until now; coupled with the reality of limited funds and difficulties in securing readily-available specialized criminological skills for such a huge and significant undertaking; the colonial GPF may now be ready for a revolutionary makeover; and Kerik is ready with his revolutionary security tool kit; to perform the nation's dance with the UK on major security changes; nothing short of a security revolution to rein in domestic terrorism, and the regional and international narcotics connection. But even any radical body security makeover may falter if crime-solving remains a political partisan affair; right now, political partisanship dictates the talking points and the 'how' on reaching solutions; enhanced in this election season.

Racial Incitement Producing a Predatory Political Culture

In recent years, we have seen the use of racial incitement to sustain a predatory political culture in Guyana. Particular political operatives, the private media, and now hate literature are the main conduits of racial provocation. All these are done, albeit in a camouflaged way, in the name of seeking political power. However, applying racial incitement not only is an illicit mechanism in the pursuit of power, but it happens within a constitutionally-approved electoral system. Power aspirants dissatisfied with the current politically-approved arrangements must know, amid their displeasure, the facts that (1) the political contenders endorsed the electoral system at the 2001 election, (2) the People's Progressive Party/Civic (PPP/C) Administration was elected under this accord, and (3) racial incitement is a violation of the rule of law.

Despite the daily dosage of racial incitement aimed at widening ethnic polarization for destabilization purposes, the masses of all ethnic groups, devoid of hatred for each other, remain undisturbed, as evidenced through their regular interactions. The UN Special Rapporteur Mr. Doudou Diène attested to this remarkable state of mind when he noted ". . .that, despite everything, this polarization, in all communities and at all levels of society, has resulted not in feelings of hatred between communities but rather in a culture of fear and mistrust which pervades all social activity. During his meetings and interviews, he also noted the existence of a sense of belonging at all levels of society. Therefore, at the basic level of the people's deepest feelings, Guyanese society does nurture the human values necessary for overcoming ethnic polarization and collectively building genuine pluralism, through which a dynamic, creative balance could enable cultural and spiritual differences to be recognized, respected, protected and promoted and universal values arising out of cross-fertilization among communities to be cultivated. . . .The story of Guyana is, to a deeply disturbing degree, the story of political exploitation of the race factor by every political leader from every point on the ideological spectrum. . . ."

Political Operatives

But we must be mindful that this ethnic polarization is not driven by the masses, but by particular political functionaries, the private media, and hate literature. The masses must be educated to know that particular political operatives exploit the race factor to gain electoral advantage. It is this political exploitation that drives mistrust and fear; the masses are not a party to this ensemble of racial agitators. For those who still are unsure about the application of racial incitement of the masses, let's provide a few illustrations.

A few examples pertaining to particular political operatives' spewing of racial hatred follow:

1. A senior People's National Congress Reform (PNCR) Central Executive member said that it "is in the business of trying to get the Government of the day out of office. There is nothing wrong with any statements which say that as an opposition party, we are attempting to remove the government."
2. The 'kith and kin' politics, referring to African ethnicity, used by the PNCR Leader at the 1997 election
3. A PNCR Member of Parliament cited the case of a senior ranking person of the PNCR, as suggesting that attacks against East Indians will produce positive outcomes.
4. The statement by the PNCR of making the country ungovernable
5. Use of the 'slow fire, more fire' phrase by the PNCR during the last election campaign
6. Allegations of a PNCR electoral candidate for the 2001 election inciting violence
7. Information on racial aspects of domestic terrorism (see GINA Website).

Media Statements

The media statements have been no different from those of the politicians. Here are just a few among many others:

1. "Government is trying to run the country by executing Blacks."
2. ". . . claims that the Government has Indo-Guyanese make-up and is totally mistaken by trying to run the country by executing Blacks."
3. "Killing of Sgt. Harry Kooseram is racially motivated. It's one for one. It's hit back time. . . ."
4. "There is a planned invasion of Buxton Village."

The incitement pieces, produced by particular political functionaries, were regurgitated over a few months in 2002 by the private electronic media. These as well as the statements emanating from the media and indeed, there are numerous others, would have a relevance in any hearing on the causes of racial domestic terrorism in Guyana, a hearing analogous to South Africa's Truth and Reconciliation Commission.

Hate Literature

Hate literature surfaced during the crime wave. Here is just one of them. "Shaka lives" and "Five for Freedom" leaflets inciting violence against Guyanese. The "Shaka lives" pamphlet sees the five prison escapees as heroes while the "Five for Freedom" leaflet indicates that the bandits have targeted all Government officials, police officers, and their families.

And indeed, we now have the Kean Gibson debacle. The Ethnic Relations Commission (ERC) currently is conducting a public inquiry into allegations of racism against the Gibson book. The book noted, among other things, that the PPP/C Government is in the throes of creating an African underclass using racial criteria. The concept of underclass may refer to people who are poor and chronically unemployed. The evidence completely belies this erroneous assertion.

People from the underclass experience a sustained social and economic disadvantage and stigma, following their dispossession of all meaningful resources. In effect, the underclass will have a low socio-economic status (SES). Let's offer just a few examples to show how Africans are doing, in order to debunk this mistaken claim.

In 2000, students with 5 or more Grade Ones at the CXC were from mixed schools with large proportions of Africans and East Indians. These were President's College, Berbice High, Anna Regina Multilateral, New Amsterdam Multilateral, Bishop's High, St. Joseph's High, Brickdam Secondary, and Queen's College. Africans compared to East Indians have relatively higher job status in the Public Service, among positions as Permanent Secretary, Deputy Permanent Secretary, Principal Assistant Secretary, Assistant Secretary, Accountant Head, and Senior Personnel Officer. Most school heads are Africans in the Nursery, Primary, and Secondary Schools. Five out of the 10 Regional Education Officers are Africans. Africans are in a majority on the State Boards in Education. At the University of Guyana, Africans constitute a majority of faculty members. Africans predominate in the disciplined forces. Data indicates that Africans receive 70% and East Indians and others 30% of house lots. Equitable budgetary provisions are allocated for African and East Indian neighborhoods.

Racial Incitement

Racial incitement is not driven by any genuine concerns for African welfare, as East Indians and Africans have comparable SES. However, racial provocation is motivated by the hot pursuit for political power via destabilization, producing a predatory political culture. The Representation of the People's Amendment Bill, No. 1 of 2001 was introduced 'to prohibit person/political parties to incite racial or ethnic violence or hatred'. It's now law and its enforcement is long overdue.

A Third Political Force not a Panacea for Guyana

"Some make-believe third force has become the new fad and foible in Guyana's politics." I made this remark about a year ago at a time when a scramble for initiating alliances became trendy. A year or so later, this initial stir of creating a third force has remained a stir, a fad, and a foible; today becoming a tenuous sculptured art form for tourist attraction.

The Times of India last year noted that the third force concept is much abused; generally promoted as an electoral emergency or out of battered egos; very unlikely to alter the body politics; sometimes the alliances are a hodge-podge of opportunistic interests; and only a grassroots foundation can make it sustainable.

The advent of new political parties does not necessarily translate into a third way or third force; and Guyana has some new parties. One of these new babyish parties is the Alliance For Change (AFC); a year ago falsely catapulted as the evolving third force. Guyana has no third force today.

Then recently, the AFC election campaign began to show Guyanese some immature Americanized public relations imprints; some false, too. But they really are a flurry of silly abbreviated political sound bites, as excitable as watching paint dry.

One AFC ad demands that all children receive immunization; clearly, the AFC is unaware that 95% of one-year-olds already are fully immunized against tuberculosis and 89% against measles (Human Development Report 2005).

Credence for the PPP/C Administration's National Master Drug Strategy Plan (NMDSP) has reached a new high; oppositional elements accord it high marks; and the AFC is no different; the AFC's crime and security plan apparently endorses some of the PPP/C's NMDSP's measures: (1)creation of a Community Policing Ministerial Unit; (2) penal reform with emphasis on correction and reintegration; (3) increase attention to vulnerable and at-risk groups; (4) gun control; (5) strengthen law enforcement agencies.

It's quite in order for other entities to endorse good measures from another party's domain, especially as these measures are in the public interest; and these PPP/C's measures have been around for more than a year; anyway, any extra endorsement can only help.

Motives

What is it that necessitates a third force? Any entity has the full constitutional right to be a third or fourth force in politics. That is not the issue. People need to examine the motives for a third force and the 'behind-the-scenes' players. People need to recall the foreign intrigue and interference in Guyana's politics in the early 1960s. Foreign intervention via the Central Intelligence Agency (CIA) in the 1960s influenced the formation of proxy groups that included Opposition political parties, the Trade Union Council, the Church, among others, to execute its violent and inhuman operations, all for the sake of removing the PPP and installing the PNC. Foreign scored a success in the 1960s, but the country paid a high price.

Look at what this foreign interference gave us—first a PNC-UF Coalition and then a PNC dictatorship. I do not want to dabble here with statistics on the Government's performance since 1992. The people will make their own judgment, a judgment that will consider the persistent orchestrated Opposition's mayhem after each election since 1992. This bedlam took its toll on the economy. People must know about this.

At any rate, any evaluation of any government has to start with a baseline. That baseline for the PPP/C Administration is 1992. I know some people are fed up with this '1992' comparison. But any evaluation of this Government requires this application. The PPP/C inherited in 1992 a very poor PNC legacy. Look at what the World Bank Group Report 1994 had to say about the PNC between 1988 and 1992:

> The government's capacity to deliver essential services has virtually collapsed. Infrastructure remains severely dilapidated. The supply of potable water is limited to a small proportion of the population, drainage and irrigation systems have deteriorated to the point that they are no longer useful, and health and education services have become so inadequate that social indicators for the country have fallen to among the lowest in the Caribbean.

During the great flood of 2005, I found it strange that Opposition operatives mouthed the 'shabbiness' of this Government's drainage and irrigation and sea defense infrastructures. It's clear from the World Bank Report these infrastructures were practically non-functional in 1992. The people need to know, too, that in the mid-1970s, these infrastructures constituted most of the Government's Capital Expenditures. In the 1980s, however, the infrastructures were perilously neglected to the point of being in a total mess. Again, it's important to review what physical infrastructures were installed after 1992 to measure their rehabilitation status.

Foreign intervention is useful only when it is non-political. And so Guyanese will need to keep a watchful eye on the prime mover and rhetoric of a third force in this country.

Third Force, an Abused Concept

In India, I read an Editorial on the third force in The Times of India, January 10, 2005 which I will like to share with you. Here goes:

Alliances Should Look Beyond Power Politics

The Third Front is a much-abused concept in Indian Politics. Even though perceived to be a platform for political parties outside the ideological space of the Congress and the BJP, it has rarely lived up to its promise. And that explains its short-lived periods in office and current irrelevance. As the CMP has rightly pointed out, a Third Front floated as part of an electoral exigency or out of bruised egos stands little chance of changing the character of the polity. The noises made by the Samajwadi Party about the need for reviving the Third Front have more to do with the Congress's refusal to accommodate it in the UPA government. The Third Front experiments in the late 80s and the 90s were successful to some extent because they were products of the times. The fragmentation of the polity which began with the decline of the Congress in the 80s empowered regional parties and opened up space for new all-India formation. The socialist remnants of the Janata Party, now united as the Janata Dal, briefly emerged as a centrist force that made it seem as if a Third political front was viable. The dust that kicked up from Mandal and mandir has now settled. After the Gujarat riots, communication of the polity has emerged as the defining issue of Indian politics. This in electoral politics translated into BJP versus Congress. The left parties, which have been consistently opposed to the Congress and the BJP in national as well as all state politics, have wisely decided to align with Congress-led UPA government for want of other possibilities.

A Third Front is now possible only if it can articulate a new politics that can be sustained by the people's movements, say on issues like right to employment, information and livelihood. The Third Front experiments all this while have been electoral alliances that were forced by the immediacies of power politics. That explains why parties like Telugu Desam, Janata Dal factions and Biju Janata Dal had no qualms in shifting their allegiances.

Long-term political alliances are workable only if they translate into grassroots politics. This would demand not just seat negotiations at the time of elections but convergence of issues of policy and governance. Such an alliance has to be organic and not a product of political maneuvering to grab power. Unfortunately, neither the Samajwadi Party nor the various outfits eyeing office in Patna seem to care. . . ."

Scrutiny

Foreign intrigue and foreign intervention in local politics need local partners to execute operations. These native partners, historically, constituted the third and fourth force that left Guyana in a sorry state. The third and possibly the fourth force of the 1960s miserably failed because of their opportunistic interests.

This type of third force is not a panacea for Guyana. Formation of a new party in itself is not a third force. A party becomes a third force in Guyana when among other things, it wins over some significant grassroots support, it has moderate leaders, it has leaders willing to negotiate their issues of policy and governance, it demonstrates its exceptionality to the main alternatives (PPP/C and the PNCR), it states what precisely it disputes with the PPP/C and the PNCR, and it is not a charade of collective opportunism. The people must do some scrutiny of this third or any 'alien' force.

It's amazing, however, that judgment already points to the viability of a third force when its platforms are not yet articulated and its 'most favored players' are caught in a maze of indecision and the waiting game.

No Return to Bondage

December 7, 1964 was an Election Day in Guyana; that day was a betrayal of trust; a time when Guyana was popular on the foreign policy agenda for both the U.S. and British Governments; its popularity birthed through U.S. and British Governments' concerns over the People's Progressive Party (PPP) Administration's perceived close ties to Moscow and Cuba. The McCarthy witch-hunt against Communism in the 1950s, and the beginnings of the Cold War shaped and engineered the U.S. Administration's concerns about Guyana. That was then!

It is said that important facts in history occur twice, first, as tragedy, and second, as farce; but now a third may occur, as purification. There always is a delay in consummating changes when a new Administration takes over; and so the time has come to remove the last institutional vestiges of PNCR-1G's economic and social tragedy; and to expose the farce of the Alliance for Change (AFC) masquerading as a third force. August 28, 2006 is another Election Day in Guyana; this day would be the day when Guyanese masses will end the last traces of the PNC tragedy, so that there is no return to bondage, the bondage of 1968-1992; the masses will reveal the true nature of the emerging AFC farce; and restore political purification in the national interest.

The PPP/C inherited a legacy of economic and social tragedy in 1992. How so? The People's National Congress (PNC) inflicted great damage to the cultural psyche of working-class Indians and Africans in Guyana through gross violations of the rule of law and their societal impact vis-à-vis fraudulent national elections from 1968 through 1985. Free speech and free press were unheard of in the Guyanese vernacular in the 1970s and 1980s. As we hit the 1970s, the National Security Act already was in place; this law suspended the right to Habeas Corpus; and gave the government powers to restrict and detain Guyanese without trial for an indefinite period. Part II of the National Security Act was reenacted in 1977 to indefinitely detain Guyanese without bail and trial. This is the kind of bondage to which we must not return.

Then there was the infamous Economic Recovery Program (ERP) that started in 1989! The ERP does not drive the PPP/C's economic strategy; the ERP was not Hoyte's brainchild. The World Bank and the International Monetary Fund (IMF) initiated the ERP through their adjustment program; and the PPP/C Administration in the 1990s negotiated significant amendments to this IMF/World Bank structural adjustment program.

What happened during the ERP years? Since the 1980s, the bauxite industry was a net user of foreign exchange coupled with high production costs. In 1988, rice production was 130,000 tonnes, with 150,000 tonnes in 1991, and 168,000 tonnes in 1992. Compare this situation with rice production of 365,000 tonnes in

1999 and 277,531 tonnes in 2005. When the PPP/C took office in 1992, sugar was imported from Guatemala. In 1989, 167,000 tons of sugar were produced. Sugar tonnage reached 321,000 in 1999 and 246,050 in 2005.

And at that time, the country was economically bankrupt. Indeed so; this is what Finance Minister Carl Greenidge said in the 1980s: "The total national savings stand at zero. . . . All appears very daunting. I can offer no comforting solution which will allow us to survive and prosper." This is the kind of bondage to which we must not return.

Think about the non-audited public service accounts over the 10 years preceding 1992; think about the external debt of US$2.1 billion; think about no revenue to service the debt in 1993; think about the 8 years from 1992 that it took to reach financial viability.

Guyana's serious economic failures and authoritarianism under the PNC dramatically curtailed active participation by all working-class Guyanese in building national unity. And so ensuring no return to bondage and make certain a brighter future for all, is the business of August 28, 2006, Election Day; no return to bondage.

Then there is the farce perpetrated by the Alliance for Change (AFC); initially presented itself as a third force. A year ago I wrote "Formation of a new party in itself is not a third force. A party becomes a third force in Guyana when among other things, it wins over some significant grassroots support, it has moderate leaders, it has leaders willing to negotiate their issues of policy and governance, it demonstrates its exceptionality to the main alternatives (PPP/C and the PNCR), it states what precisely it disputes with the PPP/C and the PNCR, and it is not a charade of collective opportunism." The AFC does not satisfy any of the eligibility criteria for a third force; the AFC has no plan for Guyana; the AFC presents sound bites as plans. This is an insult to Guyanese intelligence, and the Guyanese masses will reject the AFC for what it is, a farce. Guyana has no third force.

I added then:

What is it that necessitates a third force? Any entity has the full constitutional right to be a third or fourth force in politics. That is not the issue. People need to examine the motives for a third force and the 'behind-the-scenes' players. People need to recall the foreign intrigue and interference in Guyana's politics in the early 1960s. Foreign intervention via the Central Intelligence Agency (CIA) in the 1960s influenced the formation of proxy groups that included Opposition political parties, the Trade Union Council, the Church, among others, to execute its violent and inhuman operations, all for the sake of removing the PPP and installing the PNC. Foreign intrigue and interference scored a success in the 1960s, but the country paid a high price.

Can Guyana afford this price again? No way!

MEDIA

Whither Media: Distortions, Deceptions, and Misinformation

Concern for the political is fascinating, a good in itself, yet alarming when taking to the extremes as with so many other things. Not surprising; the election season is here. Among many of the disquieting foci is the usual resurrection of the media code of conduct seminars/workshops. And indeed the role of the state-owned media! Over the next few months, city dwellers, beware! Georgetown will showcase the tired gatherings of tribal media clansmen; why do I not just say 'clanspersons'; the usual suspects emboweled with a familiar repertoire, fully engineered to sustain sterility in the media banter, already a done deal; this charade repeats itself periodically. In spite of all previous gatherings, the five-yearly media reunions have not raised the bar for a media code of conduct for all times; a code of conduct not necessarily only for elections episodes; a code of conduct for all seasons.

This media code of conduct is serious business; examine what the media presents now, in this election season, and what the media exhibits in-between elections; more of the same. Let's take newscasts is a daily eruption of fog facts in the news, where useful information systematically fades away through opinioned newscasts; the result is a paralysis of analysis of the information; the newscasts are supposed to inform, but as Schechter (2005) aptly asserts: ". . . much of the news often disinforms, distorts, and deceives." The British newspaper the Guardian demonstrates the growing trepidation against newscasts when in a recent news quiz it published, one of the questions asked: "Who accidentally sent an e-mail to the BBC that read: "Now fuck off and cover something important you twats?"

Regular distortions and deceptions in the electronic and print media news fester and linger, when the important stories of the day are neglected or receive a biased presentation; in this way, people's misgivings about the media increase. The newscasts in Guyana, with a few notable exceptions, do not regularly depict a true picture of the day's main news stories of the country; the newscasts generally appearing as main stories from different countries rather than from one country. Several newscasts even attempt to construct and reconstruct the reality, the resultant distortion; in this construction and reconstruction process, not only distortions emerge, but important news stories are left behind.

Distortions abound too where a caption is at variance with its content. For instance, a caption in one recent newspaper issue read "PPP not 'totally satisfied' with poll preparations" is a case in point; the caption drew from the PPP's media conference last week; the conference addressed several other more objectively important issues, taking up most of the content; yet the editor decided to use this particular caption; probably because this caption is consistent with some oppositionists' position on GECOM's supposedly ill-preparations. Whatever may have been the editor's intention, the fact of the matter is that the caption was at variance with the content; and that is a distortion, overemphasizing an area that the conference hosts never intended.

There is still another side to these media distortions; excessive usage of 'Reports suggest'; 'Reliable reports state'; 'this newspaper understands' may in some cases conceal non-compliance with the verification principle. Journalists do not have to reveal their sources; but given the existing sensitivities in some stories, editors have to exercise greater vigilance where clearly excesses are being committed in the 'reliable reports state' reportage.

Again, the flood coverage is another poignant example of distortion, deception, and misinformation; ethnic tribalists were hard at work in the media in the month of January this year! Indeed distressing; especially as viewers frequently see particular ethnic groups' troubles, depending on which media house is doing the shooting; undeniably a vulgar imbalance in reporting the news.

At any rate, presenting distortions allows media houses to advance their own political agenda; invariably, the newscasts read as political broadcasts. Incontrovertibly, some media houses drive particular political lines, affording tacit support for suspecting political candidates. Anyway, media houses consider the distorted news items as important; but viewers and readers may see these news items as of no great concern, further increasing people's misgivings with the media.

Now the bells are sounding for 'equitable time' on the state-owned media. And as the election season advances, this timbre may become more vociferous. I believe the media houses in signing the Media Code of Conduct in both 2001 and 2005 endorsed equitable time for all political parties hinged on some conditionalities; make no mistake about the fact that this advocacy for 'equitable time' on the state-owned media is filled with impure waters; the belfry already is a witness to 'equitable time' afforded to many organizations, including political groupings over the years; but the bell peelers seem to have a hard time noticing this 'equitability' in action, or are even agonizing over its presence.

Even more important than 'equitable time' as a working principle of the state-owned media, is the issue of the public interest, convenience, and necessity responsibility. The public interest philosophy and responsibilities have to primarily consider program diversity; political dialog; localism; children's educational programming; access to persons with disability; and equal employment opportunity. Any discussion to improve the broadcasting media mainly focusing on 'equitable time' without holistically considering these six areas falls well short of meeting the public interest responsibilities.

Many private broadcast media houses are not fulfilling their public interest responsibilities, and really do not deserve the label 'independent'; and many violate the principles of the free press as objectivity, accuracy, and fundamental fairness. About 200 hundred years ago, President Jefferson said: "The only security of all is in a free press." And in 1823, he said: "The force of public opinion cannot be resisted when permitted freely to be expressed. The agitation it produces must be submitted to. . . ." Today, in Guyana, these statements could be re-written as: "The only danger of all is in a false media. The force of its false opinion must be rejected when permitted freely to be expressed. The agitation it produces must be refuted."

Self-censorship is a regular absentee among some journalists in this country. Self-censorship of any verbal vitriol enhances applications of fundamental fairness and may echo the sentiments of the public's interest. Therefore, a call for discussion on 'equitable time' on the state-owned media, already a 'done deal', relegates the public's interest to second place; hammering out the public's interest will unearth media distortions, deceptions, and misinformation; Are these media perversions not important enough for parliamentary discussion?

Fog Facts in the News

Concern for the political is fascinating, a good in itself, yet alarming when taken to the extremes as with so many other things.

Not surprising, the election season is here. Among many of the disquieting foci is the usual resurrection of the media code of conduct seminars/workshops. And indeed the role of the state-owned media!

Over the next few months, city dwellers, beware! Georgetown will showcase the tired gatherings of tribal media clansmen. Why do I not just say 'clanspersons', the usual suspects emboweled with a familiar repertoire, fully engineered to sustain sterility in the media banter?

Already a done deal, this charade repeats itself periodically. In spite of all previous gatherings, the five-yearly media reunions have not raised the bar for a media code of conduct for all times—a code of conduct not necessarily only for elections episodes, a code of conduct for all seasons.

This media code of conduct is serious business; examine what the media presents now, in this election season, and what the media exhibits in-between elections; more of the same.

Let's take newscasts. There is a daily eruption of fog facts in the news, where useful information systematically fades away through opinionated newscasts; the result is a paralysis of analysis of the information. The newscasts are supposed to inform, but as Schechter (2005) aptly asserts: ". . . much of the news often disinforms, distorts and deceives."

The British newspaper, the Guardian, demonstrates the growing trepidation against newscasts when in a recent news quiz it published, one of the questions asked: "Who accidentally sent an email to the BBC that read: Now f...off and cover something important you twats?"

Regular distortions and deceptions in the electronic and print media news fester and linger, when the important stories of the day are neglected or receive a biased presentation. In this way, people's misgivings about the media increase.

The newscasts in Guyana, with a few notable exceptions, do not regularly depict a true picture of the day's main news stories of the country; the newscasts generally appear as main stories from different countries rather than from one country. Several newscasts even attempt to construct and reconstruct the reality, the resultant distortion; in this construction and reconstruction process, not only distortions emerge, but important news stories are left behind.

Distortions abound too where a caption is at variance with its content. For instance, a caption in one recent newspaper issue read "PPP not 'totally satisfied' with poll preparations" is a case in point; the caption drew from the PPP's media conference last week. The conference addressed several other more objectively important issues, taking up most of the content; yet the editor decided to use this particular caption—probably because this caption is consistent with some oppositionists' position on GECOM's supposedly ill- preparations.

Whatever may have been the editor's intention, the fact of the matter is that the caption was at variance with the content; and that is a distortion, overemphasizing an area that the conference hosts never intended.

Media Distortions

There is still another side to these media distortions; excessive usage of 'Reports suggest'; 'Reliable reports state'; 'this newspaper understands' may in some cases conceal noncompliance with the verification principle.

Journalists do not have to reveal their sources; but given the existing sensitivities in some stories, editors have to exercise greater vigilance where clearly excesses are being committed in the 'reliable reports state' reportage.

Again, the flood coverage is another poignant example of distortion, deception, and misinformation, ethnic tribalists were hard at work in the media in the month January this year! Indeed distressing; especially as viewers frequently see particular ethnic groups' troubles, depending on which media house is doing the shooting; undeniably a vulgar imbalance in reporting the news.

At any rate, presenting discussion to improve the distortions allows media houses to advance their own political agenda; invariably, the newscasts read as political broadcasts.

Incontrovertibly, some media houses drive particular political lines, affording tacit support for suspecting political candidates. Any way, media houses consider the distorted news items as important; but viewers and readers may see these news items as of no great concern, further increasing people's misgivings with the media.

Now the bells are sounding for 'equitable time' on the state-owned media. And as the election season advances, this timbre may become more vociferous.

I believe the media houses in signing the Media Code of Conduct in both 2001 and 2005 endorsed equitable time for all political parties hinged on some conditionalities; make no mistake about the fact that this advocacy for 'equitable time' on the state- owned media is filled with impure waters; the belfry already is a witness to 'equitable time' afforded to many organizations, including political groupings over the years; but the bell pealers seem to have a hard time noticing this 'equitability' in action, or are even agonizing over its presence.

Even more important than 'equitable time' as a working principle of the state-owned media, is the issue of the public interest, convenience, and necessity responsibility. The public interest philosophy and responsibilities have to primarily consider programme diversity; political dialogue; localism; children's educational programming; access to persons with disability; and equal employment opportunity. Any discussion to improve the broadcasting media mainly focusing on 'equitabic time' without holistically considering these six areas falls well short of meeting the public interest responsibilities.

Many private broadcast media houses are not fulfilling their public interest responsibilities, and really do not deserve the label 'independent'; and many violate the principles of the free press as objectivity, accuracy, and fundamental fairness.

About 200 hundred years ago, President Jefferson said: "The only security of all is in a free press." And in 1823, he said: "The force of public opinion cannot be resisted when permitted freely to be expressed. The agitation it produces must be submitted to. . . ."

Today, in Guyana, these statements could be rewritten as: "The only danger of all is in a false media. The force of its false opinion must be rejected when permitted freely to be expressed. The agitation it produces must be refuted."

Self-censorship is a regular absentee among some journalists in this country. Self- censorship of any verbal vitriol enhances applications of fundamental fairness and may echo the sentiments of the public's interest.

Therefore, a call for discussion on 'equitable time' on the state-owned media, already a 'done deal', relegates the public's interest to second place; hammering out the public's interest will unearth media distortions, deceptions, and misinformation.

Are these media perversions not important enough for parliamentary discussion?

Sustaining Media Freedom

The 1970s and 1980s in Guyana may seem like many moons ago; the age of coercion where the rulers saw no limits to their authority and had the capacity to regulate all social life. Distinguished Professor Clive Thomas in an interview in 2000 (interview by Dianne Feeley and David Finkel) gave some sense of the regime in the 1970s and 1980s: "The truth however, is that this regime had been installed in power through a colonial maneuver with the electoral system before Independence in 1966, and maintained itself in power for nearly three decades through the systematic rigging of national elections and the employment of force and intimidation against all opposition to it." This was a period of intense crisis. How did the media fare in this scenario?

How can we recognize a coercive political system, or may be something approximating totalitarianism? Detection may happen through the following: a government using a total ideology to control people's lives; a single party no different from the government; extensive use of intimidation; total control of mass media; monopoly over weaponry and armed forces; and state control of the economy. Apparently, the government of the 1970s and 1980s administered a coercive political framework, or may be something authoritarian.

Free speech and free press were unheard of in the Guyanese vernacular in the 1970s and 1980s. As we hit the 1970s, the National Security Act already was in place; this law suspended the right to Habeas Corpus; and gave the government powers to restrict and detain Guyanese without trial for an indefinite period. Part II of the National Security Act was reenacted in 1977 to indefinitely detain Guyanese without bail and trial.

I want to focus on the status of media freedom depicting the political framework under which it operates, as I have just done; clearly media freedom had to be a scarce commodity within a framework of detention without bail and trial, a conduit for the government's authoritarian behavior; a scenario that ensured curtailment of media freedom to reduce dissent in the 1970s and 1980s in this country.

A recent television program examined the status of media freedom in the 1970s and 1980s, the significance for people to have access to a free media, and the status of free speech and free press today.

This program carried some pre-recorded comments of a few persons who now have expressed uneasiness to the point of dissociating themselves from that program. They claimed that the program unleashed an attack on that government's media record of the 1970s and 1980s; and these persons felt that they were misinformed on the program's purpose. Clearly, they must know that media freedom is not within the lingua franca of a coercive political system or may be something authoritarian.

Any discussion of the status of media freedom in Guyana must review its history; clearly the program did address media abuses in the 1970s and 1980s; but the program carried other dimensions too, such as, importance of access to a free media, and the sustainability of free speech and free press today.

Understanding the status of media freedom today requires understanding the history of this concept; we have to identify the social facts, aspects of social life influencing the form and content of the media; we must study the media with the same objectivity and holism as we do with education, health, economic development, etc. The media is not a sacred cow at any point in its historical development.

Some people spoke about newsprint problems and professional career difficulties on this television program. Initially, I spoke about the 'coercive' political framework, particularly encompassing the National Security law; intimidation; detention; and denial of fundamental human rights. I then presented the following:

(1) Perhaps, the government of the 1970s and 1980s perceived media control as necessary for national development and political stability;
(2) The government of the 1970s and 1980s had total monopoly of the media;
(3) the emergence of Stabroek News in the 1980s made a dent on the monopoly of the media; it has not lived up to expectations today;
(4) presented a definition of press freedom: guarantee by government to provide free speech and free press to all citizens, groups, including the

media, especially in terms of news gathering and published reporting; press freedom is not merely the right to dissent; press freedom also is an obligation to contribute;

(5) media freedom is relative, not absolute; recent cartooning of Prophet Muhammad is a violation of some people's religion, and demonstrates great disrespect for people of Islam; this is a case where media freedom becomes outlandish; there are limits to free speech;

(6) increasing prevalence of fog facts in newscasts; the result is a paralysis of analysis of information;

(7) talk-show hosts as destabilizing factor, evidenced in Whylie and Mayers' Report;

(8) Guyana in 2005 is free in relation to political rights and civil liberties, attested to by Freedom House 2005.

(9) functions of the state media – promoting government's developmental policies, programs, and projects; promoting material interest and national security; public relations campaign and media policy planner; nurturing public opinion through discussions;

(10) the media as the fourth estate, as determined by Burke; to inform and guide public opinion based on three criteria for effective media: independence, quality, and reach;

(11) the broadcast media houses need to fully comply with public interest, convenience, and necessity responsibilities;

(12) abuse of press freedom today.

The television program was intended to highlight media restrictions in Guyana's history and to ensure that whatever we do, we must strive to sustain free speech and free press. In this context, I explained the growing and urgent need for a broadcasting law and a broadcasting authority to quell the lingering media insanity and media perversion in current broadcasting.

At all times, we must ask two questions about the media as Noam Chomsky does: what are the media houses attempting to do? And what effects do media houses have on the public? The answers will differ at different points in a country's history; the different answers historically are important for analysis; answers that are significant, necessary and perhaps sufficient to developing the media algorithm for a plan of corrective action.

The Media is not Sacred

The media is not sacred; media activities have boundaries, limitations, not a free for all; no media house is above the law. And anyone has the right to challenge the media.

Note that in 2004 the U.S.-based Freedom House rated Guyana a free country, strong on political rights and civil liberties.

Countries experiencing transitional democracy have few private media; Guyana reeks of private media, not surprising given the Freedom house rating.

Every day, media houses attempt to evaluate the society's performance, an appraisal invariably not meeting the standards of objectivity, accuracy, and fundamental fairness.

Partisan political sentiments each day drive some private media. In some ways, these private media houses place a higher priority on partisan political interests than on the national agenda.

A few years ago, Caribbean Communications Specialists Dwight Whylie and Harry Mayers of the Independent Media Monitoring and Refereeing Panel, commenting on Guyana's media, indicated that talk shows have degenerated and were a 'significant destabilizing factor' in the society.

Media Monitors Whylie and Mayers also criticized one talk-show host saying that the information put out was 'unsubstantiated allegation or accusation, much of it defamatory and likely to fan the flames of distrust, prejudice and discontent.' They asserted that the allegation was irresponsible in a fragile democracy and inimical to nation building. Some print media too are equally guilty of peddling half-truths.

Media editors and owners in question need to reassess their existing over-politicized orientations and consider an ethical approach to presenting news and opinions. 'Out-of-control' reporting and opinions over-politicize the society.

Freedom of Speech & Freedom of the Press

The concepts of freedom of speech and freedom of the press are not absolute, for they have to be applied within the law and rules of society. Article VIII of the Charter of Civil Society for the Caribbean Community stipulates that there should be freedom of expression and access to information. But the Charter went on to say that exercise of this right requires special duties and responsibilities, and may be effected subject to reasonable restraints for the public good, as may be rationalized in law in a democratic state.

Prime Minister Basdeo Panday in 1998 remarked "I do not believe that freedom of the press includes the untrammelled right to publish lies, half-truths and innuendoes about anyone." Even the most liberal Western democracy requires restrictions on these two fundamental rights in the public interest.

In 1997, Dr Michael P. Mortell, President of The National University of Ireland, said that freedom of the press is not an absolute. He further argued that the French Declaration of Rights, and several international rights instruments, such as, the Irish Constitution, the European Convention for the Protection of Human Rights and Fundamental Freedoms (1950) or the UN International Covenant on Civil and Political Rights (1966), all include freedom of speech, but do not bestow a privileged status on the Press. The Press is not sacred.

The U.S., as one of these liberal Western democracies, has strong statutory measures to deal with 'hate' speech and other racist 'bias' statements, and acts. Currently, 40 States in the U.S., excluding Wyoming, have a hate crimes law; these measures do encroach on freedom of the press and freedom of speech. So is Article 20 of the International Covenant on Civil and Political Rights.

Guyana's Constitution, too, espouses this freedom as a right and as an obligation through Article 146 (1) and (2), including being a signatory to the Declaration of Chapultepec.

Some media operatives carry on their charade as if the people of this country are not knowledgeable and capable, unable to think for themselves. Everything is reduced to politics. They use an unsavory 'quantum leap' tool to draw flimsy conclusions and thereby sustain their particular twisted points of view. The media charades with their distorted conclusions continue in the quest to demoralize, over-politicize, and destabilize the society. One of the goals of over-politicization via media lies is to destroy human free will, producing gullibility to such lies, creating victims in the process.

On the face of it, as people seem to become captives to these outlandish and non-evidentiary-based media conclusions, are we saying that the people have no choice over their own behavior, or are their actions only shaped by these infectious tirades that today fill the political and media landscape of this country? The fact that these twisted media diatribe push people into a resistance mode, is powerful evidence that their warped discourses may not have the effect they claim to have.

People's behavior determines what they become as individuals, developing a capacity to change society. You see a person's identity is formed in society, the media playing its part; but the media does not totally influence people's behaviors. If people merely accept all that the media puts out, then clearly those media houses would have won the day. Fortunately, human behavior has the capacity to agree and disagree, to accept and reject, to oppose dubious limitations. To the dismay of the media fraternity, people can and do make choices, a choice to resist a constant bombardment of media perversion. Control of this media perversion eventually will come from the people.

Race, Ethnicity, and the Media in Guyana

People entering the media field in Guyana need to understand the social context of the society on which they will report. Interpretations grounded in an understanding of social contexts tend to be objective, reliable, valid, and fundamentally fair. One of the dominant characteristics of the Guyana social context is the perception of racism and racial discrimination. Therefore, a major thrust among media operatives is to examine the society's multiethnic character historically and contemporaneously on the media.

Media in a Position of Dominance

A good grounding in the multiethnic character of the society, both historically and contemporaneously, will enable us to examine the media role and its involvement in presenting distorted communication. The media, today in Guyana, can be viewed as the central nervous system of society. The media occupy a position of dominance in our culture and politics, as never seen before. The media houses are ubiquitous, and could well be on the way to saturate

Guyanese lives. Media houses play a daily role in attempting to influence the governing process in Guyana. Every day, the media evaluate the Government's performance. These daily evaluations aspire to inform and mobilize Guyanese continuously. If they are successful in these efforts, then they are managing public sentiment. Clearly, too, there are professional biases among journalists, for they tend to have preference for items that spotlight recognizable patterns of race and ethnic conflict, action, and drama. The reported items, generally, have a visible and distinct protagonist.

The Media as a Socialization Agent

The media, acting as an agent of socialization, help to form a person's identity. This process is achieved through a person's contact with the 'media culture' that presents a large frame of reference. A person's identity is an emerging consciousness. Consciousness refers to internal cognitive and emotional awareness inherent in each individual that mainly arises from learning experiences (Real, 1996:38). In the media, the person creating the media message conceives of it in the messenger's own consciousness. The media message is, then, transferred via a medium to become an experience in the consciousness of the receiver. The person, conceivably, could develop a distorted consciousness and social identity when media reports are consistently biased. In this case, the receiver may be viewing the world with inaccurate lens.

As a socialization agent, the media have to mirror the society. Are the media really objectively and accurately reflective of Guyanese society in the area of race and ethnic relations they interpret race conflicts in the context of class stratification? The answer is no. Most electronic and some print media present biased and extreme media messages consistent with their particular political party affiliation or sympathy, without regard to objectivity, accuracy, and fundamental fairness.

Media Making Wrong Decisions - Media Distortions

The media sometimes commit Type I and/or Type II Errors (Medler and Medler, 1996:175-177). Type I Error is a wrong decision made to reject a statement of no relationship or no difference between two or more factors. In effect, a conclusion is made that a difference or relationship between the factors exists, when in fact it does not. Type II Error is a wrong decision to accept a statement of no difference or relationship between variables, concluding that no difference or relationship between the factors exists when in fact it does. An example relevant to Guyana is where the media houses are regularly committing Type I Error. This particular Type I Error refers to an erroneous conclusion drawn where ethnic conflict between Africans and East Indians is determined as being nationwide. If this were so, then all multiethnic societies are racially unstable because they have this countrywide ethnic conflict. This is not the case, since many of these countries are relatively stable as evidenced by their high levels of social and economic development. The U.S. as a multiethnic society is a good example of relative stability. Pockets of institutional racism and discrimination are ever present and, of course, they have to be addressed. But pockets of institutional racism are not tantamount to a nationwide racial divide and ethnic conflict.

Let's explore the Type I Error through this notion of Guyana having nationwide racial divide between Africans and East Indians, in order to demonstrate media distortions political commentaries claim that racism is rampant in Guyana, and the elected People's Progressive Party (PPP)/Civic Government only represents East Indian interests.

The People's National Congress (PNC) Party claimed that the 1997 elections were rigged, and as such, refused to acknowledge the PPP/Civic Administration, including the President. The political commentaries claim, too, that the PNC represents African interests. What has emerged since the last two elections, say the commentaries is a sharpened polarization of the two races-Africans and East Indians. Allegations of racism constitute the main theme of these political commentaries. Undoubtedly, racism is alive and well in Guyana as it is in most multiethnic societies. But is such racism equivalent to a nationwide racial divide producing nationwide ethnic conflict and violence?

Guyanese across racial and class lines are concerned with having stable employment and job security, rising real wages, access to quality and affordable health care, quality education, and child care, strategic areas where discriminatory practices can be sought. The evidence does not support the view that nationwide discrimination encroaches on each of these institutions, to the point where Africans are treated in an inferior way, or East Indians are denied rights on the basis of their race.

In education, both Africans and East Indians have comparable rates of high school attendance, high school graduation, and access to higher education. With regard to jobs, Africans are conspicuous in the higher echelons of the public service to which they have traditionally gravitated. Inadequate access and quality health care are found throughout the society to which both poor Africans and East Indians are vulnerable. The current Minister of Health is providing a tremendous boost to the nation's health status.

In the pursuit of eliminating racism and ethnic conflict, a key indicator is racial discrimination is an act of unfair treatment directed against a person on the basis of that person's perceived racial characteristics. Invariably, a person who suffers racial discrimination is perceived by the discriminator (individual, institutions) as someone who is inferior due to his/her race discrimination has to be identified and measured, in order to demonstrate the extent of racism in Guyana level of discrimination can be identified through an indicator called 'socioeconomic status' (SES). SES is a combined index score pertaining to education, income, and occupation. If Africans are the victims of large-scale racial discrimination, then they would have a lower SES, compared to East Indians, at each class level. Again, if East Indians were subject to considerable discrimination, then their SES would have been lower than that of Africans at each class level. But this is not the case for both groups. In fact, Africans and East Indians have comparable SES, since they are well represented in each class division.

Media commentaries, in alluding to racism in Guyana, must provide evidence as to how the two major ethnic groups are affected by racism and discrimination when they have comparable SES. However, institutional discrimination does exist in the corridors of some institutions, and these have to be addressed by the People's Progressive Party/Civic (PPP/Civic) Administration. But given the comparable SES of both Africans and East Indians at each class level, the media characterization of Guyana being racially polarized on a nationwide scale, is a gross distortion, and therein lies the Type I Error. The 'letters' section in Stabroek News is a case in point.

Stabroek News' Letters on Ethnic and Race Relations - A Case Study in Media Distortion

Stabroek News continues to give space to the incessant finger pointing between the two major ethnic groups in Guyana. Invariably, with hindsight, ethnic history can be interpreted to support a particular position, without any grounding in scientific scholarship. This is socially irresponsible, as this finger pointing while merely an exercise in intellectual rhetoric, possibly serves the newspaper's purpose of fanning the flames of hatred. In this futile intellectual bravado, each party to the dialog wants to win his/her argument.

This approach smacks of a zero-sum power game where a person always wins at someone's expense. Pro-East Indian commentators want to present a positive side to their argument, and Africans have a similar goal. This is certainly not the process for enhancing race relations in a multicultural society. Finger pointing, historically, is a popular activity among ethnic extremists course, they are found on both sides of the ethnic camps. Guyanese from all walks of life must reject this extremist line, as it is inimical to social development. Stabroek News allegedly seems to be playing one ethnic group against the other in the same way the imperialists divided these two ethnic groups.

Stabroek News does this very well by allowing space to anxious opportunists and ethnic extremists, in order to lay the groundwork for ethnic and political instability. In so far as these finger pointing exercises persist, the Guyana society will be perceived as being unstable.

This appears to be the goal of Stabroek News. In effect, ethnic extremists are quite functional for Stabroek News. Whatever travesty might have been committed by both groups, let's not remind each other as to which group has the highest score on perversion. What really is anyone's motive for wanting to determine who scored the highest in human atrocities?

The ethnic scorecard perspective is applied here. For instance, for a few days in any week, letters present a particular ethnic viewpoint, and the score at that time may be, say 2-0. On the other days of that week, letters will represent another ethnic perspective, and so the score at that point may be 2-4. The scorecard panorama is unnecessary, and most of the time the letters present redundant data. This approach certainly cannot contribute to progressive race and ethnic relations.

However, we need to understand the social context in which some outrage of inhumanity occurred. Let's not forget that the entire framework for any abomination in Guyanese history, was socially engineered by external forces. The hands of both major ethnic extremist groups in Guyana are stained with the blood of inhumanity to man and hatred of fellow Guyanese extremists are peddling their brand of racist pollution, and Stabroek News is a tremendous facilitator. Of course, the newspaper may say that this is what free speech is all about. But such public discourse must be conducted within the norms and parameters of social responsibility.

In determining content for public dissemination, the good of the society must supersede any individual's self-interest and opportunistic tendencies. Guyana is a multicultural society that socially regresses amid such inappropriate public dialog. Guyana is a pluralist society based on mutual respect among the many ethnic groups for one another's cultures. Ethnic extremism pollutes this healthy pluralism and advances racial hatred. The finger pointing debate fails to understand its role in socially reconstructing the ethnic hatred landscape. Significant intra-ethnic differences prevail for both Africans and East Indians. Ethnic extremists seem unable to perceive these changes in 'Indianness' and 'Africanness'. Their sterile debate can only see ethnic groups as static. In another context, Anna Maria Arias of Hispanic magazine would classify this finger-pointing debate as, "It's stupid. There are more important issues we should be talking about"

In this multiethnic society, panethnicity has appeared. Panethnicity is the growth of solidarity among ethnic subgroups. Coalition of different ethnic groups to promote a cause in the interests of a specific region would be an example of panethnicity. Fundamental cultural differences among East Indians themselves are predominantly highlighted by East Indian ethnic extremists, in order to show strength in the Indian diversity. But they use a sterile method to assess 'Indianness', and, therefore, cannot see the emerging panethnicity among East Indians. Some African ethnic extremists also promote significant variations among Africans, and so are unable to visualize, too, a creeping panethnicity among Africans. In effect, ethnic extremists' perceptions pertaining to the ethnicity of Africans and East Indians are not similar to the perceptions on ethnicity held by both Africans and East Indians.

Solidarity within East Indian and African subgroups reduces the potency of ethnic extremism, and therefore, produces an opportunity to improving race and ethnic relations. Ethnic extremism thrives on the cultural differences within a particular ethnic group. Some have been exploiting this situation in the name of free speech. However, panethnicity within each ethnic subgroup has the capability to reduce the spread of ethnic extremism, the dreaded social disease.

While Stabroek News may claim that they are facilitating free speech by disseminating all ideas, their constant presentation of ethnic extremism in the letters' section, defies the boundaries of reasonableness, fundamental fairness, and an irresponsible understanding of race and ethnic issues. Therein lies the media distortion. How can Stabroek News claim to be an objective conduit for the distribution of all ideas when some of those ideas inaccurately, unfairly, and aggressively promote Indianness to the detriment of Africanness and Africanness to the disadvantage of Indianness, within the social context of a multiethnic society?

This line of thinking by Stabroek News, apparently, smacks of a promotion of hate speech. Those who defend the letters' section of Stabroek News, due to lustful political blinkers, may not be able to see the ethnic hate that is churned out daily. Or maybe they do! Extremists' arguments in favor of these hate writings are also not surprising because Stabroek News provides a convenient site for these misguided people to spew their literary filth in the public sphere. The concepts of freedom of speech and freedom of the press are not absolute, for they have to be activated within the parameters of the law and the normative rules of society. Media protocols and a code of conduct generally, can correct some of these media distortions.

The criticism made of Stabroek News is not that the newspaper fails to allow the inclusion of normative free speech, but that it promulgates 'ethnic and extremist' materials which assault the dignity and humanity of both major ethnic groups in Guyana. A content analysis of the letters included, based on the scientific method, will almost certainly reveal findings that do not reject the assertion of its inaccurate, unfair, inflammatory, and degrading presentation of the history and culture of Africans and East Indians. Let Stabroek News put this claim to the test by assembling competent behavioral and social science researchers, to conduct such a study. Indeed, Stabroek News will be obligated to fund this research program! This study will definitively support the claim of media distortions in the letters' section on race and ethnic relations in Stabroek News.

Striving for Undistorted Communication

Media should contribute to nation building by helping to produce a society with undistorted communication. The purpose of this kind of media presentation is communicative understanding (Ritzer, 1996:155). The media can achieve communicative understanding through a process of consensus. Consensus itself is reached through discourse, but only when four validity claims are recognized by media houses. These are:

- The media presentations are understandable.
- The media statements are true, that is, media houses are presenting reliable knowledge.
- The media houses are reliable.
- The media houses have the right to make these statements, provided that the other three claims are met.

However, Guyanese, since the December 1997 national elections, have witnessed various forces that prevent this consensus from unfolding, resulting in a high volume of distorted media communication.

Freedom of Speech & Freedom of the Press

The concepts of freedom of speech and freedom of the press are not absolute, for they have to be presented within the law and the normative rules of society. Article VIII of the Charter of Civil Society for the Caribbean Community stipulates that there should be freedom of expression and access to information. But the exercise of this right requires special duties and responsibilities, and may be effected subject to reasonable restraints for the public good, as may be rationalized in law in a democratic state.

Prime Minister Basdeo Panday remarked "I do not believe that freedom of the press includes the untrammeled right to publish lies, half-truths and innuendoes about anyone" (Speech in Parliament, 1998). Even the most liberal Western democracy requires restrictions on these two fundamental rights. The U.S., as one of these liberal Western democracies, has strong statutory measures to deal with 'hate' speech and other racist 'bias' acts.

Responsible Reporting

The Herdmanston Accord alluded to the creation of a new environment in which conflict resolution can be effected with agreed procedures by both major parties, without the use of accusatory language and distorted communication that may inflame the political context. Media houses must be required to present responsible reporting, for their role is significant in contributing to progressive race and ethnic relations. Responsible reporting requires objectivity, accuracy, and fundamental fairness.

Multiculturalism, a Key to Guide the Media

The history of the Caribbean has shown the biased role media houses have played in reporting and analyzing race conflicts vis-à-vis invariably and covertly supporting ruling political parties, especially those parties that thrive on inflaming racist sensitivities. Sometimes, the media do it under the guise of promoting free speech addition, media houses usually present the notion of racism and discrimination unlinked to class. Using this perspective will not bring real solutions to race and class conflicts. In so far as any dominant ethnic party attempts to assimilate the other ethnics to its value system, the race politics will endure.

The media by bolstering this evil brand of politics can only add credibility to this sinister development. Those harnessed with political power in the Caribbean must ensure the sustenance of other people's cultures, and therefore focus policy agenda on the principle of multiculturalism. Effecting such policies would not only develop a culture of trust, but would obliterate the need for race politics. In this scenario, the media would have no choice but to use the idea of free speech in the name of multiculturalism.

The Caribbean has remained and functioned at or below the poverty line for far too long, largely as a result of the mistrust fostered among ethnic groups in each class category. Government's policy frameworks grounded in real multi-culturalism will carry positive seeds for the creation of a nation. Individual Car-ibbean societies will not become real nations as long as its politicians continue to dabble in race politics. Governments with assistance from media houses will have to provide leadership in the promotion of multiculturalism.

Copyright Provisions Exist in Guyana

Guyana has copyright provisions!

It is, however, true to say that we have no local statute on copyright. But Guyana is a signatory to the Berne Convention and the Universal Copyright Convention. In addition, other copyright legal provisions are enacted in the Copyright Act 1956 of the United Kingdom to which Guyana acceded in 1966.The problem, however, is that these copyright provisions are not enforced.

In 1988, Guyana, in order to receive beneficiary status under the Caribbean Basin Initiative, had to be a signatory not only to the Berne Convention, but also a signatory to the Universal Copyright Convention.

Copyright is a type of protection provided by law to authors of original works of authorship, inclusive of literary, dramatic, musical, artistic, and some other intellectual works. Let's now take a snapshot view of the Berne Convention and the Universal Copyright Convention.

The Berne Convention

Guyana is among 121 countries that were party to the Berne Convention on March 2, 1997. These countries are as follows:

Albania, Argentina, Australia, Austria, Bahamas, Bahrain, Barbados, Belgium, Benin, Bolivia, Bosnia and Herzegovina, Brazil, Bulgaria, Burkina Faso, Cameroon, Canada, Central African Republic, Chad, Chile, China, Colombia, Congo, Costa Rica, Côte d'Ivoire, Croatia, Cuba, Cyprus, Czech Republic, Denmark, Ecuador, Egypt, El Salvador, Estonia, Fiji, Finland, France, Gabon, Gambia, Georgia, Germany, Ghana, Greece, Guinea, Guinea-Bissau, **Guyana**, Haiti, Holy See, Honduras, Hungary, Iceland, India, Ireland, Israel, Italy, Jamaica, Japan, Kenya, Latvia, Lebanon, Lesotho, Liberia, Libya, Liechtenstein, Lithuania, Luxembourg, Madagascar, Malawi, Malaysia, Mali, Malta, Mauritania, Mauritius, Mexico, Monaco, Morocco, Namibia, Netherlands, New Zealand, Niger, Nigeria, Norway, Pakistan, Panama, Paraguay, Peru, Philippines, Poland, Portugal, Republic of Korea, Republic of Moldova, Romania, Russian Federation, Rwanda, Saint Kitts and Nevis, Saint Lucia, Saint Vincent and the Grenadines, Senegal, Slovakia, Slovenia, South Africa, Spain, Sri Lanka, Suriname, Sweden, Switzerland, Thailand, The former Yugoslav Republic of Macedonia, Togo, Trinidad and Tobago, Tunisia, Turkey, Ukraine, United Kingdom, United Republic of Tanzania, United States of America, Uruguay, Venezuela, Yugoslavia, Zaire, Zambia, Zimbabwe

The Berne Convention is based on three principles, as follows:
- Works created in one contracting country must be afforded the same protection in each of the other contracting countries as these give to the works of their own citizens. This is the principle of no discrimination.
- The copyright protection is unconditional. This is the principle of automatic protection.
- The copyright protection is independent of the availability of protection in the country where the work originated. This is the principle of independence of protection.

With regard to original works, the protection will comprise "every production in the literary, scientific and artistic domain, whatever may be the mode or form of its expression" (Article 2(1) of the Berne Convention.

The Berne Convention contains 38 Articles as follows:
- Article 1 [Creation of Union]
- Article 2 [Literary and Artistic Works Covered]
- Article 2*bis* [Legal Proceedings / Press Reports]
- Article 3 [Nationality of Authors and Coverage]
- Article 4 [Nationality and Motion Pictures or Architecture]
- Article 5 [National Treatment; Formalities Forbidden]
- Article 6 [Dealing with Nationals of Countries Outside the Union]
- Article 6*bis* [Moral Rights}
- Article 7 [Duration]
- Article 7*bis* [Joint Authorship]
- Article 8 [Right of Translation]
- Article 9 [Right of Reproduction]
- Article 10 [Fair Use]
- Article 10*bis* [News Coverage]
- Article 11 [Right of Performance]
- Article 11*bis* [Right of Broadcast]
- Article 11*ter* [Right of Public Recitation]
- Article 12 [Right of Adaptation]
- Article 13 [Sound Recordings]
- Article 14 [Cinematographic Rights]
- Article 14*bis* [Protection of Cinematographic Works]
- Article 14*ter* [Inalienable Rights in Original Works]
- Article 15 [Proof of Authorship]
- Article 16 [Seizure of Infringing Works]
- Article 17 [Censorship]
- Article 18 [Works Covered When the Convention Takes Effect]
- Article 19 [Right to Claim Greater National Protection]
- Article 20 [Relationship to Other Treaties]

- Article 21 [Appendix Provisions Dealing with Developing Countries]
- Article 22 [The Assembly]
- Article 23 [Executive Committee]
- Article 24 [The International Bureau]
- Article 25 [The Union's Budget]
- Article 26 [Amendment of Articles 22-26]
- Article 27 [Revision]
- Article 28 [Ratification and Accession]
- Article 29 [Accession by Countries Outside the Union]
- Article 29*bis* [Countries Not Bound by Articles 22-38]
- Article 30 [Effect of Ratification or Accession]
- Article 31 [Application to Territories]
- Article 32 [Effect on Earlier Convention and Its Revisions]
- Article 33 [Disputes Among Countries]
- Article 34 [Effect on Earlier Convention and Its Revisions]
- Article 35 [Leaving the Union]
- Article 36 [National Measures to Enforce]
- Article 37 [Official Texts]
- Article 38 [Countries Not Bound by Articles 22-26]

Each of these Articles should mandatorily be reviewed in the preparation of a copyright draft for legal enactment in Guyana.

What rights are protected through the Berne Convention? These rights are to be interpreted as rights of authorization, and they are:

- right to translate
- right to make revisions and arrangements of the work
- right to publicly perform in drama, and musical works
- right to publicly narrate literary works
- right to communicate to the public the presentation of such works
- right to broadcast
- right to make reproduction in any way
- right to utilize the work as the origin for an audiovisual work
- right to demand authorship of the work and the right to demur any mutilation, or any offensive action against the work, which would compromise the author's character and standing.

Copyright protection generally lasts through the life of the author plus 75 years. However, copyright protection for audiovisual or cinematographic works continues until 50 years after the work was made public. For applied art and photographic works, copyright protection is, at least, 25 years from the date of origination of the work.

The Universal Copyright Convention

The Universal Copyright Convention was adopted at Geneva in 1952 through the sponsorship of UNESCO, and took effect in 1955.

Some facets of it are as follows:

- No signatory country should give its own local authors more favorable copyright treatment than the authors of other signatory countries.
- An official copyright sign must be inscribed in all works and have the symbol ©, the copyright owner's name, and year of first publication.
- The minimum duration for copyright protection must be the life of the author plus 25 years, excluding photographic works and applied works, which must have a 10-year protection.
- Signatory countries must afford an exclusive right of translation for seven years.

The Universal Copyright Convention has an incisive philosophical basis. This philosophy takes the view that a system of copyright protection suitable for all countries and presented in a Universal Convention, will guarantee individual rights and promote the growth of literature, the sciences, and the arts. In addition, a universal copyright system will produce an increased dissemination of information and advance international understanding.

Both Conventions considered the needs of developing societies with regard to translation, reproductions, public performances, and broadcasting. So at a Paris Conference in 1971, both the Berne Convention and the Universal Copyright Convention eased up regulations in the areas of teaching, scholarship, and research for developing countries.

Guyana needs a local statute on copyright to provide protection within its own legal system. But whatever statute is created, that statute must conform to the international standards as stipulated through the Berne Convention and the Universal Copyright Convention. For instance, the Berne Convention some years ago increased protection to the life of the author plus 75 years. The US Copyright Law is likely to revise its current 'life plus 50 years' into compliance with international standards as indicated in the Berne Convention.

Any broadcasting law, in making provisions for copyright, also must comply with international standards through the Berne Convention and the Universal Copyright Convention, or ant other appropriate international conventions.

The need for a copyright law in Guyana is urgent. A draft of copyright provisions is currently being studied within the Attorney's General's Office, and hopefully some movement will now be effected.

Gecom Media Monitoring: Some Lessons to be Learnt

Responsible reporting requires accuracy, balance, and fundamental fairness, and a compliance with the principles and ethics of journalism. In this vein, the first Guyana Elections Commission (GECOM) Media Monitoring Project prior to the 2001 election, was strategically timed to vitiate the lunacy that passes for journalism in Guyana.

Today, many broadcasting stations and broadcasters do not fulfill their civic and legal responsibilities. Broadcasters have entered into an almost sacred pact with the public, given that broadcasters obtain an exclusive use of public property—the spectrum. In return, broadcasters agree to serve the public interest.

However, precious few broadcasters comply with the public interest principle, to the point where news coverage and talk show content have lost meaningful dimensions. Balanced and accurate news coverage and talk show materials are such rare phenomena that they should be placed on the endangered species list.

The GECOM Media Monitoring Unit (GMMU) Reports prior to the 2001 election, while an important first step to correct deficiencies in the broadcasting world, seemed to have engaged, perhaps unwittingly, in methodological adventurism.

The mandate of the GMMU was to inform citizens in a pre-election environment about the behavior of the media and to inform the media themselves about their own behavior. This being the case, then, GECOM had a serious responsibility to present valid and reliable information. Validity and reliability to ascertain scientific integrity of GMMU cannot be determined merely by visiting GECOM's offices, as was presumed in the past. The GMMU reports presented for public dissemination, in their own right, also must have details substantiating their own scientific integrity. Visiting GECOM's offices should not be a prerequisite for determining scientific integrity.

The objective in evaluating the GMMU Reports was to assess their worth based on the validity of the projects as reported. The relevant literature, as related to the Caribbean and Guyana, was not presented. The authors of these Reports, also, should have synthesized the literature, related theoretical models, their experiences, and their perceptions of the problem. This synthesis is required, so as to provide a rationale for this line of research.

GMMU's methodology now will have to draw from several disciplines. Future Reports emanating from GMMU must contain an appropriate methodology section, and not merely a laundry list of definitions styled as 'methodology', as shown in previous reports. Providing mere definitions by themselves does not constitute 'research methodology'.

The consequence is that many methodological questions would remain unanswered. For instance, in relation to the previous GMMU reports, I am not convinced that the coding used in the content analysis included the logic of conceptualization and operationalization. Also, if a monitor examined all news stories within a particular period, then the monitor would need to give us a sample of them, so that we can assess the appropriateness of the coding utilized.

GMMU needed to present all news items reviewed, perhaps, appendicized, so we could have ascertained whether they objectively pertain to the three categories used: political parties, GECOM, or Government. The Reports did not provide this information, essential for assessing and evaluating the monitoring project.

In addition, we need to have a general working agreement on the use of these terms. GMMU also needs to indicate the operations utilized to measure these specific concepts. In addition, the Methods section, also, should indicate the standards used to classify news items into 'positive', 'neutral', and 'negative'.

The Reports acknowledged relying on methods used by media professionals in many monitoring projects worldwide. The GMMU Reports may have very well done that, but these methods were vaguely presented.

In any case, it is simplistic to conclude that because GMMU's method was previously applied in Eastern Europe and elsewhere, it necessarily follows that such a method can be fully utilized here. We constantly have to refine and modify research methods to ensure that our research design is appropriate for a new society. The previous GMMU Reports did not demonstrate that this procedure was followed. This research protocol must be applied in the future.

The GMMU Project in the 2001 election was based on a reactive approach whereby the monitoring process was driven daily by political party platforms and events, rather than the concerns of voters. The information, therefore, generated in this process, did not enable the voter to make an informed choice. The information should have been grounded in voters' concerns and issues.

The use of 'Government' with regard to election-related matters in the news coverage, constituted another problem. Outside of its legislative mandate, the Government has no business in dabbling with election matters. The Government does not contest an election, a political party does.

GMMU used 'Government' as a category in the media monitoring process in Guyana. In fact, reputable media monitoring bodies do not use 'Government' as a category in democracies.

Let me now address the state media in Guyana. Unlike many countries experiencing transitional democracy, Guyana is one of the few that has an abundance of private media interspersed with the state media. Every day, the private media attempt to evaluate the Government's performance, and this evaluation does not always comply with the norms of objectivity and fundamental fairness.

The state media in this context have to continue to promote nation-building projects.

Again, for the state media, no distinction was made between reports on Governmental programs and projects, and election-related items. Given this blurred distinction, the GMMU erroneously suggested that the state media provided a high positive coverage for the Government. This coverage for Government seemed to include both facts for Governmental projects mixed with election-related matters.

Media monitors need to understand the salient role of the state media in Guyana, as they were the targets of disparagement by previous GMMU Reports. The Voice of America, Radio Marti, and Radio Free Europe/Radio Liberty, all funded by the U.S. Congress, promote foreign policy positions of U.S. Administrations. These are some of the U.S. state media that collectively are a mouthpiece for U.S. foreign policy. The Guyana state media are not that different. The Guyana state media promote, among other functions, the nation building policies, programs, and projects of Government.

Monitoring of the media during an election campaign in Guyana, with a history of rigged elections, is a politically sensitive activity. In order to apportion credibility and integrity to this type of media project, it is absolutely necessary, therefore, inter alia, to summarize the parameters of the training program used, and to publicize the staff profiles of the monitoring unit.

The GMMU Project's integrity must be discerned through its own transparent structure and functions. Therefore, validity and reliability of any GMMU Project's findings will have to be determined through the public documents issued, and not through conducted tours at GECOM's Media Monitoring Unit.

Inject a Public Trustee Model in Broadcasting Now

"Freedom of the press implies freedom to write headlines. But I presume that freedom of the press also implies public responsibility…I am aware that sensational headlines sell newspapers. They are bad enough when they are dealing with sex and crime. But they are far worse when they are likely to cause disaffection in the public service." These are statements Dr. Cheddi Jagan made in 1958 and 1959 about the print media. Today, some print media still seem to have an aversion to uphold public responsibility.

Media Lawlessness

Now we have some electronic media that carry on as if they have no public responsibility, as evidenced by the Media Monitoring report of 2001 and general media statements that approximate media lawlessness.

Dwight Whylie and Harry Mayers monitored the media scene from February 1 through March 25, 2001 in Guyana. They referred to one broadcast as: ". . . dangerous mischief which violates many tenets of professional journalism and several clauses of the Media Code of Conduct." They referred to talk shows as a "significant destabilizing factor" in Guyana. I previously presented numerous irresponsible media statements spewed out during the crime wave 2002-2003. Regrettably, the media lawlessness today has graduated to a form of entertainment in this country.

Use of Airwaves

Several media operatives continuously violate the terms and conditions for use of the electromagnetic spectrum. This spectrum is a scarce national resource, and is not owned by any individual talk show host, television station, or other agency. The licensee, invariably the owner of the television station, agrees to comply with the terms and conditions of the spectrum. The spectrum is issued under license by the National Frequency Management Unit (NFMU).

The recent suspension of CNS 6 from transmitting and the ensuing enforcement of that suspension, has once again brought into play intentional confusion between freedom of speech and loss of license, due to alleged non-compliance with the terms and conditions of the spectrum. In this perplexity, freedom of speech again has transiently become the guardian of the license, implicitly making the licensee's agreement with the NFMU a secondary affair. 'Yes' to freedom of speech, but a similar 'Yes' to compliance with the NFMU's conditions, must be acknowledged. Generally, it's untidy to want freedom of speech and simultaneously not want to comply with the NFMU's conditions. The Advisory Committee on Broadcasting (ACB) as an advisory body is expected to advise the Minister on compliance issues by Television Station Licensees on licensing conditions and to advise the Minister on appropriate action in the event of non-compliance with such licensing conditions and other related functions. At any rate, the Minister has the right to agree or disagree with any recommendation from this advisory entity. And indeed the comparison of the ACB with the Federal Communications Commission (FCC) is way out of line; it's not even close!!

The Public's Concerns

Let's now talk about how we can inject the public's concerns in broadcasting, as these concerns are fast becoming customized agendas for particular interest groups. Make no mistake that broadcasting is considered a sacred cow for some television station managers in Guyana. Clearly, little consideration is given to the public interest, convenience, and necessity. Discussions on regulation of broadcasting have to start from a premise of the people or the public's interests and needs. However, broadcasters, by accepting as their most important responsibility, the need to serve the public interest, convenience and necessity, can implicitly create a 'public trustee' model. U.S. broadcasters are required to comply with such a public trustee model. The Federal Radio Commission depicts the 'public trustee' model as follows: "[Despite the fact that] the conscience and judgment of a station's management are necessarily personal . . . the station itself must be operated as if owned by the public. . . . It is as if people of a community should own a station and turn it over to the best man in sight with this injunction: "Manage this station in our interest." The standing of every station is determined by that conception."

In the U.S., the public's concerns are addressed through the public trustee model in the following six areas: program diversity; political dialogue, localism; children's educational programming; access to persons with disabilities; and equal employment opportunity. Here, I shall try to show how the U.S. developed this public interest standard in broadcasting through source materials drawn from the National Telecommunications and Information Administration (NTIA).

Program diversity: This diversity first implemented in 1929 mandated the station to meet the: "tastes, needs and desires of all substantial groups among the listening public . . . in some fair proportion, by a well-rounded program. . . ." (Great Lakes Broadcasting Co. v. FRC, 37 F.2d 993 (1930). A market approach to public interest was applied in the 1980s. But today, both the Congress and the FCC have realized that using the market approach alone to achieving the public interest is wanting.

Political dialog: Public interest responsibility also has to do with political candidates and citizens' access to broadcasting. The Zapple Rule requires that equal airtime must be available for all political candidates, excepting political editorial advertising. The Fairness Doctrine, which tried to ensure that all sides are presented fairly, was rescinded in 1987 because it was deemed to be inimical to public interest. However, other measures, as the Fourteenth Amendment to the Constitution and the Civil Rights Legislation, are in place to compensate for the elimination of the Fairness Doctrine.

Localism: The Blue Book in 1946 indicated two requirements for promoting localism. These were 'local live programs', and 'programming devoted to discussion of local public issues'. The 1960 Program Policy Statement endorsed two requirements: 'opportunity for local self-expression'; and 'the development and use of local talent'.

Children's educational programming: Congress ratified the Children's Television Act in 1990, which mandated broadcasters to have three hours of educational children's programming per week, catering to children 16 years and under. The law further restricted children's advertising to 12 minutes per hour during weekdays and 10.5 minutes during weekends.

Access for persons with disabilities: The Television Decoder Circuitry Act of 1990 mandates all television sets to carry special decoder chips to display closed captioning on television programs. Section 305 of the Telecommunications Act of 1996 introduced more requirements for the deaf and hard-of-hearing.

Equal Employment Opportunity: The FCC must assure that licensees meet the needs and interests of minorities and women, and to make certain, too, that an appropriate number of minorities and women are employed by the broadcast stations. Broadcast stations do not meet the public interest obligations if they fail to provide equal employment opportunities.

Self-regulation in Guyana

National discussion on the regulation of broadcasting in Guyana started 'one hundred' or many years ago. Then we saw the Joint Committee on Radio Monopoly, Non-Partisan Boards and Broadcasting Legislation. Defining these discussions were some partisan sections of the media world that earnestly believe that broadcasting should be self-regulated. They further believe that even if there is little or no self-regulation, then the Parliament and not Government should drive the major decisions for the composition, functions, and operations of a broadcasting authority.

The American experience demonstrates that self-regulation and leaving the market forces alone to serve the public's interest, convenience, and necessity in broadcasting are inadequate. Both the market and self-regulation mechanisms can play a role in broadcasting, but the Government and Parliament through a broadcasting authority must establish the minimum requirements for the public's concerns as well as general broadcasting principles.

Talk-Show Hosts - A Significant Destabilizing Factor

Unlike many countries experiencing transitional democracy, Guyana is one of the few that has an abundance of private media interspersed with the state media. The private media, particularly through talk-show hosts, play a daily role in attempting to influence the governing process in Guyana. Every day, the private media attempt to evaluate the Government's performance, but this evaluation does not always comply with the norms of objectivity and fundamental fairness.

Talk-show hosts of the private media ilk may be quite fine, if their reporting is value—free and conform to some semblance of objectivity. But they are not.

As you relate to the broadcast, print, and electronic media each day, it is obvious that many private media houses, through these talk-show hosts, are driven by partisan political sentiments. In some ways, these private media houses place a higher priority on partisan political interests than on the national agenda.

Dwight Whylie and Harry Mayers of the Independent Media Monitoring and Refereeing Panel (IMM&RP), both prominent Caribbean Communications specialists, indicated in their second report, that talk shows have degenerated and were a 'significant destabilizing factor' in the society.

The IMM&RP found Clem David's Sunrise Show to be obnoxious and statements spurted out as lacking in evidence. Clem David claimed in his response that talk-show hosts do not have to provide evidence. Whylie pointed out that for any talk-show host to claim that it was not his/her responsibility to provide evidence, was sheer illiteracy, as all information has some foundation for truth. The notion of talk-show hosts not wanting to seek out the evidence, is dangerous and irresponsible, according to Whylie.

Media Monitors Whylie and Mayers also criticized Mark Benschop for broadcasting several expletives in a conversation with Police Commissioner Laurie Lewis. The Panelists believe that this broadcast violated the code of ethics in journalism. The independent Panelists confirmed that Benschop's information is 'unsubstantiated allegation or accusation, much of it defamatory and likely to fan the flames of distrust, prejudice and discontent. In our view this is grossly irresponsible in a volatile political climate leading to general election'.

Most Codes of Ethics in broadcast journalism require journalists to collect and report information of importance and interest to the public accurately, honestly and impartially. Talk show hosts' main purpose of presenting an opinion or commentary is to inform the public and help them to make judgments on the issues of the day. Talk show hosts' opinions and commentaries must be held to the same standards of accuracy with regard to facts as news reports. Clearly, Codes of Ethics in journalism support Whylie's position, that talk-show host Clem David in not providing evidence for his remarks on the Sunrise Show, violated the public trust. Talk-show hosts need to be reminded that they do not own the electro-magnetic spectrum; the airwaves are a national asset, in that it is owned by the people.

The Representation of the People's Amendment Bill, No. 1 of 2001 was introduced 'to prohibit person/political parties to incite racial or ethnic violence or hatred'. Yet, on a nightly basis, we see a few talk-show hosts heaping mountains of verbal assaults on persons and groups, assaults that may be construed as racist, or as incitement to ethnic violence. A sample of Clem David's remarks made on Saturday, March 3, 2001, follows:

- 'Millions of dollars to buy people who work at GECOM'; this was a reference made to the PPP/C.
- 'There is a command center at UNDP and Pegasus Hotel'.
- 'Operatives inside UNDP office being paid to rig election'.
- The truck that brought stones to the recent Tucville political meeting belonged to a prominent PPP/C individual.

Incidentally, Clem David certainly is not the only talk-show host that violates the norms of professional journalism.

Some talk-show hosts recently have addressed the national ID cards, legally to be used for voting. Guyanese of many different political persuasions and ethnicity, as of today, still have not received their ID cards. However, these talk-show hosts present the issue as if only PNC/Reform supporters are intentionally denied access to these cards. Whether or not, talk-show hosts' inflammatory remarks on the ID cards may have led to the street protests over the last two days, will only be discerned through a comprehensive investigation. At that time, GECOM was exerting tremendous efforts to ensure that the distribution of these ID cards was completed in a timely manner. I think it is time that all Guyanese and the political parties show trust and confidence in GECOM, an independent constitutional agency. Give GECOM a chance to function appropriately, so that it can swiftly remove the chinks in the electoral process.

The State Media, a Mouthpiece for Nation Building Projects

I want to address the private media first in this viewpoint. Today, these media agencies operate in a position of dominance in our culture and politics, as never seen before. The media houses are ubiquitous, and may very well be on the way to saturate Guyanese lives. They play a daily role in attempting to influence the governing process in Guyana day, the media attempt to evaluate the Government's performance, and this evaluation does not always comply with the norms of objectivity and fundamental fairness. These daily evaluations try to continuously inform and mobilize Guyanese. If they are successful in these efforts, then they are managing public sentiment. This is what we perceive of the private media today.

These activities of the private media may be quite fine, if their reporting is value—free and conform to some semblance of objectivity. But they are not. Most recently, one of the dailies, on its front page, carried a wholly inaccurate story on GBC; every element in the story was untrue, and it smacks of sloppy journalism. This is just one of many examples of the private media presenting inaccurate stories on the PPP/C Administration and its agencies. As you relate to the broadcast, print, and electronic media each day, it is obvious that many private media houses are driven by partisan political sentiments. In some ways, these media houses place a higher priority on partisan political interests than on the national agenda, as seen through developmental outcomes.

Against this background of fundamentally unfair private media reporting and blatant vulgarity masqueraded as journalism, it is important that the state media—GBC, GTV and the Guyana Chronicle—act like today's spokesperson for developmental projects and outcomes contributing to the national agenda.

Given the attempt by other media houses to manage public sentiment through presenting erroneous information periodically, we cannot depend solely on private media to disseminate information on developmental projects objectively.

Among the responsibilities of our state media, may be the following:

- The state media are expected to expose the public, both nationally and internationally, to the country's developmental efforts that contribute to nation building.

- The state-media's mission is to promote material interest and national security through informing the public by presenting consistently Government's philosophy, policies, programmes and projects.

- The state media perform the role of public relations and media policy planner. In this way, the state media administer public relations campaigns on national agenda items, such as,

HIV/AIDS, anti-narcotics, environmental issues, democracy, gender and ethnicity matters, housing, education, etc.

- The state media present policies and developmental programs clearly and effectively, and also provide responsible discussions and opinions on these policies.

- The state media represent Guyana, not a single segment of Guyanese society, and so are expected to give a balanced and comprehensive projection.

Officials governing some state media around the world have used repressive sanctions and political pressures against journalists. Clearly, state media in such brutal environments are not free.

However, the Guyana media, including the state media, are considered free, as determined by the Press Freedom Survey 1999. And any broadcasting authority that is established to regulate the media, will have jurisdiction over both state and private media.

A better understanding of the role of the state media is necessary; the state media are not the mouthpiece of the People's Progressive Party/Civic state media are the spokesperson for developmental programs, essential to nation building.

Race

Rodney on Race

Twenty-five years ago today a tarnished historical legacy was birthed in Guyana, then a land of horrors. During the evening of Friday, June 13, 1980, Walter Rodney was assassinated.

Today's Perspective will examine Rodney's work on race as a contradiction among the working class during indenture. For a long time, ordinary people in this country have had little say in race matters; only the 'high-browed' seem positioned to articulate their distorted positions on race issues. This review on race matters, therefore, is timely where ordinary people's lens reach new highs in Rodney's intellectual prism.

Seeing the history of a situation largely from the point of view of working people and not solely from the ruler's perspective helps an individual to reach validity and reliability with greater integrity. But to make this happen means workers must develop a stock of knowledge.

In this context, Rodney sees history as a vehicle to presenting knowledge which ordinary people can use. Eventually, these same ordinary people and others can apply this knowledge to produce change to better their lives. Rodney vigorously applied this perception of history to ground with the working people. Let's see how Rodney uses his view of history, through providing greater credence to working people's lens, to explain the perception of race in 19th century British Guiana (now Guyana).

Indian Arrival from the Ruled Perspective

On the question of race, this Rodneyite grounding produces a multiplicity of explanations on the Indian arrival in British Guiana in 1838. Most of the 'politically correct' explanations for Indian immigration, that is, explanations solely from the rulers' perspective, border on a labor shortage and cheap labor. But there were other explanations, too, derived from the ruled point of view.

The White planters' (rulers) reason advanced for inducing Indian immigrants to Guyana was to fill a labor void. The rationale was as follows: African slaves were emancipated and left the sugar plantation in droves, thereby creating a labor shortage. The freed slaves demanded increased wages. Planters refused. And the Indian Diaspora was born.

The ordinary people (freed slaves) and Indians later explained the Indian presence differently. Indian immigrants did not fill any labor void. Freed slaves numbered about 100,000 in 1830, and, therefore, were in adequate numbers to effectively man the sugar plantations. However, planters wanted a different kind of worker to Africans, a worker to be recruited as bound labor.

Under conditions of bound labor, planters exercised total control over the worker; the indentured worker was bonded to work on a particular sugar plantation over a 5-year period, with a fixed pay averaging 24 cents or a shilling per day or $1.50 as average weekly earning, no physical mobility from the estate without permission, and to be forced out from the 'logies' to work whenever the necessity arises, among other harsh conditions.

Planters also explained that the immigrant labor was cheaper than to have continued with large numbers of freed Africans on the plantations. The freed Africans rejected the planters' reasons and suggested that even if they had won higher wages, the plantation expenditure would have turned out to be less than the total cost of immigration. The planters' position, perhaps, was deceptive.

Manager Bascom of Plantation Cove and John noted in 1903 that planters' contribution to immigration increased their wage bill by 25 percent. Edward Davson in evidence to the Sanderson Commission in 1910 claimed that when the cost of sugar production was $50 per ton, immigration costs were $4.80 per ton. Clearly, planters' labor shortage and cheap labor as pretexts did not provide the full story for importing indentureds. The freed African story seemed to offer greater integrity as an explanation of the passage from India.

Change for Human Betterment

Rodney tried to explain a situation from the working people's point of view. In this vein, genuine change for human betterment will only occur through knowledge accrued mainly from working people's lens. This thinking has unfolded in Guyana's history. How?

Early perception of race was indistinguishable for Creoles and immigrants, according to Rodney. But the working people in the 19th century began to see that their objective conditions were incompatible with the planters' reading of the situation. That was change in the making. Let's further review the situation.

Rodney posits that planters in a multiethnic society would encourage an exaggeration of racist perceptions solely with the view to postpone the creation of working class unity. One of the biggest problems Africans had with Indian indentureds was the threat of employment. And, indeed, too, that whole episode of White planters' displacement of African small farmers with Indian small farmers created a unique legacy of racial acrimony. In that situation, planters offered Indians lands in lieu of their repatriation passages to India.

Notwithstanding this highly-charged situation, Minutes of the Court of Policy in November 1880 showed that Africans expressed concerns where the police and prison services were strengthened to contain Indians; in anti-immigration positions, Africans were keen to point out that they bore no ill will against Indians, but that they opposed the conditions of their arrival and the vile consequences of indenture; and Dwarka Nath in A History of Indians in British Guiana noted that freed Africans gave evidence to substantiate the view that the first Indian arrivals experienced similar conditions as African slaves.

Rodney said "Although planters were willing to exploit racial differences, none of the African- Indian clashes of the 19th century came anywhere close to large-scale communal violence. . . . Their common deprivation was a bond; and at the same time these two races had not developed any relations of mutual exploitation." The fact of the matter was that planters as the ruling class then faced two working-class struggles, one waged by the freed slaves and the other by the indentureds and other Indians, largely a result of the fundamental unity of interests between Indians and Africans. These struggles eventually closed the gaps in the pursuit of working-class unity. This, indeed, was genuine change taking place.

Racial division overstated

Notwithstanding the race contradictions that still plague this country, Guyana's history is not inundated with racial conflict but ethnic alliances. However, some politicians and the private mass media want us to believe that race-ethnic conflict pervades this land. Rodney makes the point that the case advanced of highly prevalent racial conflict in the society is inaccurate. This is what he has to say:

> . . . my contention is that the case for the dominant role of racial division in the historical sphere has been overstated, and that scholarship on the subject has accepted without due scrutiny the proposition that Indians and Africans existed in mutually exclusive compartments. The problems of interpretation lie not only in the marshalling of the evidence, but, more fundamentally, in the historical methodology that is applied.

Rodney shows that the cultural legacies of both Indians and Africans have not played a role in race conflict in Guyana. However, both the planters of the 19th century and contemporary politicians have used a manipulative strategy for political control of the masses. This strategy has worked to mask both Indian and African cultural identities as well as a basic unity of their interests. The cultural legacies of both major ethnic groups are a precondition for national unity.

A Scientific Understanding of Race and Ethnic Relations in Guyana

The Guyana society has experienced excessive rhetorical battering on race relations problems over the last nine years, to the point of naivety. The seeds of racial and ethnic discord were sown in the British colonial era, with revitalized reinforcement in the 28 years of the Burnham/Hoyte Administration up until 1992.Much has been done in the PPP/Civic governmental period since 1992 to address racial discrimination issues. More work, integral to dealing with these concerns, however, has to be effected.

Three reasons are advanced by Cross to explain why a society characterized by diverse ethnic origins, and with British colonial experience, would, indeed, display racial problems. Firstly, in the colonial period, race as a factor was used to classify the colonized; secondly, the belief in the inequality of the human races was applied to maintain the social order; and finally, the effect of the Westminster model with its emphasis on the two-party system, is certain in societies like Guyana, with two major ethnic groups, to produce racial cleavages. The first two reasons historically have been substantiated.

The third reason, that is, the Westminster model, is tainted with superficiality, has not been validated. An implication of the third reason is that a change in the parliamentary system from a 2-party model to a system of power sharing, would resolve race issues. Numerous parliamentary changes in multiracial societies have not brought about the desired changes in race relations.

The United States Congressional system is a good case in point. With all the democratic elements enshrined in Congress and the Constitution reinforced by Congressional concern for justice and equality, the U.S. still remains inherently a racist society. Racism heaped upon vulnerable minorities in the U.S. will not be fully resolved by effecting changes in the Congressional system.

Parliamentary systems are mere conduits for the protection of vested power interests in the society. The credibility of this remark can be clearly seen in works that address the question, "who governs America?" Chances are that political systems could make meaningful resolution to racism, but only if the people are the architects of the parliamentary system. Political systems are shaped by the dominant class interests of society. So it is not the parliamentary system, but the roots of inequality that primarily are targeted to address race relations problems.

Race problems derived from inequality, are grounded in the class base of society, and must be resolved through focusing on an interaction among race, class, and ethnicity attempt to address race and ethnic issues must include, firstly, a baseline understanding of all ethnic groups' socioeconomic status (SES) which comprises education, occupation, and income/wealth. This baseline data will identify strategic areas of racial discrimination that need a plan of corrective action. The corrective action will be policy interventions that are class-race-ethnicity driven.

We also need to understand conditions under which the various ethnic groups came to Guyana, and the nature and type of their interaction in their different social classes, over these many years. In this regard, some strategic questions need to focus the discussion on an interaction among class, race, and ethnicity which could be the basis for policy formulation in any Equal Opportunities Commission. Four strategic questions in race and ethnic relations, as applied by Marger, are:

- The nature of intergroup relations. Here, we assess the levels of competition, conflict accommodation, and cooperation among all ethnic groups in Guyana.

- The ranking system of ethnic groups. Evaluate the extent to which ethnic groups are treated differently and given unequal amounts of valued resources to do with education, occupation, and income (SES).These resources refer to wealth, prestige, and power. What the consequences of unequal and different treatment mean for different ethnic groups, can be determined.

- The methods used by the dominant ethnic group to maintain its position at the top of the political and ethnic hierarchy. Determine whether the dominant ethnic group uses prejudice and discrimination to sustain its power interests. What attempts are made to maintain a system of ethnic inequality, could be a useful area of inquiry.

- The long-term outcomes of relations among these ethnic groups. Consider whether the ethnic groups are moving toward pluralism or assimilation, or combinations of these. Examine the social forces that support any of these potpourris.

- Underlying these four questions are the following statements on racism, as outlined by Marger:

- Racist thought accepts that differences among groups are innate, and unlikely to change.

- Racist thought is ethnocentric. People with racist ideas see ethnic out-groups as inferior, and any interaction with them will result in a degeneration of their group.

- Racist thought does not mirror reality; it is mythical. Over time through frequent usage, the racist thinking becomes accepted as beliefs, values, and norms of society.

- Racist thought is prevalent where physical differences are quite visible.

The proposed Equal Opportunities Commission could use this framework appropriately to the benefit of all Guyanese. To date, no serious study of race and ethnic relations, based on the scientific method, focusing on the four questions has been administered in Guyana, numerous critical remarks on racism in Guyana, are frequently made in the media, commentaries that are unsubstantiated and lacking scientific integrity. Policy formulations have to be grounded on reliable and valid data.

This Commission will need a research and a social action component, using the scientific method. A database on racial discrimination can evolve through the research process. In fact, in an incidental sense, a macro study that is, indeed, urgent is to examine the social psychology of voting. This study is long overdue, as all the premature politicians preaching impending doom out of a false concern for resolving racism, revisit the racial turf at election times.

In this electoral 'race' climate, self-appointed protectors of East Indians perceive themselves to be more 'Indian' than those who reject their 'medicine' for Guyana. The same can be said for self-appointed protectors of Africans. This type of behavior is a political farce.

Let us engage in fruitful endeavors, applying scientific tools, to understand the state of race and ethnic relations in Guyana, and stop this naive race rhetoric.

Racial Incitement Producing a Predatory Political Culture

In recent years, we have seen the use of racial incitement to sustain a predatory political culture in Guyana. Particular political operatives, the private media, and now hate literature are the main conduits of racial provocation. All these are done, albeit in a camouflaged way, in the name of seeking political power. However, applying racial incitement not only is an illicit mechanism in the pursuit of power, but it happens within a constitutionally-approved electoral system. Power aspirants dissatisfied with the current politically-approved arrangements must know, amid their displeasure, the facts that (1) the political contenders endorsed the electoral system at the 2001 election, (2) the People's Progressive Party/Civic (PPP/C) Administration was elected under this accord, and (3) racial incitement is a violation of the rule of law.

Despite the daily dosage of racial incitement aimed at widening ethnic polarization for destabilization purposes, the masses of all ethnic groups, devoid of hatred for each other, remain undisturbed, as evidenced through their regular interactions. The UN Special Rapporteur Mr. Doudou Diène attested to this remarkable state of mind when he noted ". . . that, despite everything, this polarization, in all communities and at all levels of society, has resulted not in feelings of hatred between communities but rather in a culture of fear and mistrust which pervades all social activity. During his meetings and interviews, he also noted the existence of a sense of belonging at all levels of society. Therefore, at the basic level of the people's deepest feelings, Guyanese society does nurture the human values necessary for overcoming ethnic polarization and collectively building genuine pluralism, through which a dynamic, creative balance could enable cultural and spiritual differences to be recognized, respected, protected and promoted and universal values arising out of cross-fertilization among communities to be cultivated...The story of Guyana is, to a deeply disturbing degree, the story of political exploitation of the race factor by every political leader from every point on the ideological spectrum. . . ."

Political Operatives

But we must be mindful that this ethnic polarization is not driven by the masses, but by particular political functionaries, the private media, and hate literature. The masses must be educated to know that particular political operatives exploit the race factor to gain electoral advantage. It is this political exploitation that drives mistrust and fear; the masses are not a party to this ensemble of racial agitators. For those who still are unsure about the application of racial incitement of the masses, let's provide a few illustrations.

A few examples pertaining to particular political operatives' spewing of racial hatred follow:

1.   A senior People's National Congress Reform (PNCR) Central Executive member said that it "is in the business of trying to get the Government of the day out of office. There is nothing wrong with any statements which say that as an opposition party, we are attempting to remove the government."
2.   The 'kith and kin' politics, referring to African ethnicity, used by the PNCR Leader at the 1997 election
3.   A PNCR Member of Parliament, cited the case of a senior ranking person of the PNCR, as suggesting that attacks against East Indians will produce positive outcomes.
4.   The statement by the PNCR of making the country ungovernable
5.   Use of the 'slow fire, more fire' phrase by the PNCR during the last election campaign
6.   Allegations of a PNCR electoral candidate for the 2001 election inciting violence
7.   Information on racial aspects of domestic terrorism (see GINA Website).

Media Statements
The media statements have been no different from those of the politicians. Here are just a few among many others:

1.   "Government is trying to run the country by executing Blacks."
2.   ". . . claims that the Government has Indo-Guyanese make-up and is totally mistaken by trying to run the country by executing Blacks."
3.   "Killing of Sgt. Harry Kooseram is racially motivated. It's one for one. It's hit back time. . . ."
4.   "There is a planned invasion of Buxton Village."

The incitement pieces, produced by particular political functionaries, were regurgitated over a few months in 2002 by the private electronic media. These as well as the statements emanating from the media and indeed, there are numerous others, would have a relevance in any hearing on the causes of racial domestic terrorism in Guyana, a hearing analogous to South Africa's Truth and Reconciliation Commission.

Hate Literature
Hate literature surfaced during the crime wave. Here is just one of them. "Shaka lives" and "Five For Freedom" leaflets inciting violence against Guyanese. The "Shaka lives" pamphlet sees the five prison escapees as heroes while

the "Five For Freedom" leaflet indicates that the bandits have targeted all Government officials, police officers, and their families.

And indeed, we now have the Kean Gibson debacle. The Ethnic Relations Commission (ERC) currently is conducting a public inquiry into allegations of racism against the Gibson book. The book noted, among other things, that the PPP/C Government is in the throes of creating an African underclass using racial criteria. The concept of underclass may refer to people who are poor and chronically unemployed. The evidence completely belies this erroneous assertion.

People from the underclass experience a sustained social and economic disadvantage and stigma, following their dispossession of all meaningful resources. In effect, the underclass will have a low socio-economic status (SES). Let's offer just a few examples to show how Africans are doing, in order to debunk this mistaken claim.

In 2000, students with 5 or more Grade Ones at the CXC were from mixed schools with large proportions of Africans and East Indians. These were President's College, Berbice High, Anna Regina Multilateral, New Amsterdam Multilateral, Bishop's High, St. Joseph's High, Brickdam Secondary, and Queen's College. Africans compared to East Indians have relatively higher job status in the Public Service, among positions as Permanent Secretary, Deputy Permanent Secretary, Principal Assistant Secretary, Assistant Secretary, Accountant Head, and Senior Personnel Officer. Most school heads are Africans in the Nursery, Primary, and Secondary Schools. Five out of the 10 Regional Education Officers are Africans. Africans are in a majority on the State Boards in Education. At the University of Guyana, Africans constitute a majority of faculty members. Africans predominate in the disciplined forces. Data indicates that Africans receive 70% and East Indians and others 30% of house lots. Equitable budgetary provisions are allocated for African and East Indian neighborhoods.

Racial Incitement

Racial incitement is not driven by any genuine concerns for African welfare, as East Indians and Africans have comparable SES. However, racial provocation is motivated by the hot pursuit for political power via destabilization, producing a predatory political culture. The Representation of the People's Amendment Bill, No. 1 of 2001 was introduced 'to prohibit person/political parties to incite racial or ethnic violence or hatred'. It's now law and its enforcement is long overdue.

Shaping Indian Politics through Indian Worker Resistance
Part 1

The abolition of slavery brought freedom to about 80,000 slaves; but this freedom would not have seen the light of day had it not been for African resistance. Slave revolts in Barbados in 1816, in Demerara in 1823, in Jamaica in 1824, in Antigua in 1831, and again in Jamaica in 1831 together with the Anti-Slavery Movement, and fluctuating sugar profits, created the ingredients for the Abolition of Slavery Act in 1834. And by 1848, the African peasant class of villagers emerged. Around 1850, Indians replaced slaves on the sugar plantations, taking on the distinctiveness of a new rural working class; Indian resistance throughout the 19th century challenged the might of the planters' oligarchy and the colonial parliament, where each uprising, riot, or discontent laid the foundations for more disturbances, and where each disorder unleashed new dynamics in their quest to undermine the imperialist stranglehold.

By the 1850s, the slave-owning plantocracy came to an end. And limited liability companies became the new owners and controllers of the sugar plantations. But Indian resistance, constant sugar crises, the freeing up of crown lands in 1898, and the 1891 constitutional reform enabling the electorate to choose legislators, were pivotal forces advancing the final demise of a decaying planters' oligarchy. The focus in this paper is to show how Indian resistance shaped Indian political evolution in this country; note that Indian working people were the key architects of this persisting resistance during indenture; and not the petty Indian merchants and the educated Indian middle class who were in awe of the plantocracy. They demonstrated great inclinations to assimilate the planters' value system and generally accepted and complied with cultural imperialism.

Planters' control over labor was total under slavery; with the end of slavery, plantation owners yearned for a 'controllable' labor force as a surrogate for slaves on sugar estates. British plantation owners believed that India fitted the bill; India's huge population was a ready-made labor pool; labor with agricultural skills; and India, a British Colony, negating the need for negotiations with foreign authorities. Indian arrival to the sugar plantations of the Caribbean as indentureds under such rationale became a reality, initiating in Hugh Tinker's words, 'a new system of slavery'.[1]

Indentureship gave total control of labor to planters; indentureship prohibited any individual or collective bargaining; and during indenture, strikes were deemed 'uprisings' or 'disturbances'. A further enhancement of total control emanated through Ordinance Number 9, 1868 where wages were not released if planters determined the indentured's work to be incomplete or unsatisfactory. In fact, this Ordinance produced and reproduced the most telling and recurrent complaints by Indian indentureds.

Indentured Indians inhabited a dehumanized total institutional environment, with no mobility, enslaved by the tyranny of the rule of law, and reduced to a history of humiliation parallel to conditions of African slavery; the neo-slave nature of indentureship is well established.[2]

White planters, Colored, and African lower status groups loathed the Indian culture, thus: "Their language was 'outlandish', they knew no English; their clothes were strange and their religion was heathen. They lacked the cultural characteristics valued in the society, and in return the society withheld its rights and privileges from them."[3] Indians arrived in the Caribbean as outsiders and remained as 'outsiders' even today.

Given the harsh treatment meted out to Indians, how did they manage to maintain their culture? The answer has to do with their resistance and resilience. Their resistance to the White planters was a rallying point for cultural continuity and the genesis of Indian political evolution. Just a few examples would substantiate that Indian resistance was a characteristic feature of plantation life. Indians staged 88 strikes and disturbances between 1886 and 1888,[4] and they received 65,084 convictions for labor contract violations between 1874 and 1895.[5]

In 1881, 3,168 were labeled criminals because of their struggles with planters. In fact, compared to other British Colonies, British Guiana became the worst offender where planters used the criminal courts to enforce labor laws, as evidenced in the table for 1907:[6]

Table 2.1: Indentured Adults & Convictions in 1907

	Indentured Adults	Convictions under Labor Laws (no. %)
British Guiana	9,784	2,019 (20%)
Trinidad	11,506	1,869 (16%)
Jamaica	2,832	237 (8%)
Fiji	10,181	2,091 (20%)
Mauritius	47,000	1,492 (3%)

Disaffection among both indentured and unindentured Indians produced intermittent violence representing one pole on the range of Indian assertiveness; their disaffection created the germ for political activism. In 1872, low wages at Plantation Devonshire Castle produced mass protests where police shot and killed five and wounded seven workers. The *Parliamentary Papers, No. 49* of 1873 claimed that Oederman, a Brahmin (upper caste), was the instigator of this uprising. Planters believed that upper-caste Indians were the source of constant instigations on the estates. The Sugar Planters' Association even urged immigration authorities in Calcutta in 1889 not to recruit upper-caste Indians; and Alleyne Ireland, an overseer, referred to these upper castes as '. . . incorrigible rascals, sowing the seeds of discontent. . . .'

Rigid labor laws produced criminal convictions for the slightest violations. Medical doctors and magistrates operated in the ruling class interests, once they were paid off handsomely. Indian women became frequent targets for sexual assaults by White overseers. Although arrests were common, Indians continued to resist. There was the case in January 1882 of Narain Singh[7] who went to the Immigration Agent-General (IAG) to lodge a complaint pertaining to his wages; he was advised to present his complaint to a magistrate; this he did and the magistrate then invited the manager of Plantation Providence to review Narain Singh's complaint. The manager summoned Narain Singh and told him he was under an indenture contract and that he left the job to proceed to the Immigration- Agent General (IAG) without appropriate permission; the magistrate then dismissed the case.

Notes

1. Tinker, Hugh. *A New System of Slavery: The Export of Indian Labor Overseas, 1830-1920.* Oxford, 1974.
2. Nath, Dwarka. *A History of Indians in British Guiana.* London, 1950, p. 16.
3. Jayawardena, Chandra. *Conflict and Solidarity on a Guianese Plantation.* London, 1963, p. 17.
4. Comins, D.W. *Note on Emigration from India to British Guiana.* Calcutta, 1893, p. 96.
5. Ireland, W. Alleyne. *Demerariana.* Georgetown, 1897.
6. *The Sanderson Commission.* Parliamentary Papers. 27, 1910, p. 13.
7. Court of Review, 1882.

Shaping Indian Politics through Indian Worker Resistance
Part 2

The abolition of slavery brought freedom to about 80,000 slaves; but this freedom would not have seen the light of day had it not been for African resistance. Slave revolts in Barbados in 1816, in Demerara in 1823, in Jamaica in 1824, in Antigua in 1831, and again in Jamaica in 1831 together with the Anti-Slavery Movement, and fluctuating sugar profits, created the ingredients for the Abolition of Slavery Act in 1834. And by 1848, the African peasant class of villagers emerged. Around 1850, Indians replaced slaves on the sugar plantations, taking on the distinctiveness of a new rural working class; Indian resistance throughout the 19th century challenged the might of the planters' oligarchy and the colonial parliament, where each uprising, riot, or discontent laid the foundations for more disturbances, and where each disorder unleashed new dynamics in their quest to undermine the imperialist stranglehold.

By the 1850s, the slave-owning plantocracy came to an end. And limited liability companies became the new owners and controllers of the sugar plantations. But Indian resistance, constant sugar crises, the freeing up of crown lands in 1898, and the 1891 constitutional reform enabling the electorate to choose legislators, were pivotal forces advancing the final demise of a decaying planters' oligarchy. The focus in this paper is to show how Indian resistance shaped Indian political evolution in this country; note that Indian working people were the key architects of this persisting resistance during indenture; and not the petty Indian merchants and the educated Indian middle class who were in awe of the plantocracy. They demonstrated great inclinations to assimilate the planters' value system and generally accepted and complied with cultural imperialism.

Planters' control over labor was total under slavery; with the end of slavery, plantation owners yearned for a 'controllable' labor force as a surrogate for slaves on sugar estates. British plantation owners believed that India fitted the bill; India's huge population was a ready-made labor pool; labor with agricultural skills; and India, a British Colony, negating the need for negotiations with foreign authorities. Indian arrival to the sugar plantations of the Caribbean as indentureds under such rationale became a reality, initiating in Hugh Tinker's words, 'a new system of slavery'.[1]

Indentureship gave total control of labor to planters; indentureship prohibited any individual or collective bargaining; and during indenture, strikes were deemed 'uprisings' or 'disturbances'. A further enhancement of total control emanated through Ordinance Number 9, 1868 where wages were not released if planters determined the indentured's work to be incomplete or unsatisfactory. In fact, this Ordinance produced and reproduced the most telling and recurrent complaints by Indian indentureds.

Indentured Indians inhabited a dehumanized total institutional environment, with no mobility, enslaved by the tyranny of the rule of law, and reduced to a history of humiliation parallel to conditions of African slavery; the neo-slave nature of indentureship is well established.[2]

White planters, Colored, and African lower status groups loathed the Indian culture, thus: "Their language was 'outlandish', they knew no English; their clothes were strange and their religion was heathen. They lacked the cultural characteristics valued in the society, and in return the society withheld its rights and privileges from them."[3] Indians arrived in the Caribbean as outsiders and remained as 'outsiders' even today.

Given the harsh treatment meted out to Indians, how did they manage to maintain their culture? The answer has to do with their resistance and resilience. Their resistance to the White planters was a rallying point for cultural continuity and the genesis of Indian political evolution. Just a few examples would substantiate that Indian resistance was a characteristic feature of plantation life. Indians staged 88 strikes and disturbances between 1886 and 1888,[4] and they received 65,084 convictions for labor contract violations between 1874 and 1895.[5]

In 1881, 3,168 were labeled criminals because of their struggles with planters. In fact, compared to other British Colonies, British Guiana became the worst offender where planters used the criminal courts to enforce labor laws, as evidenced in the table for 1907:[6]

Table 2.2: Indentured Adults & Convictions in 1907

	Indentured Adults	Convictions under Labor Laws (no. / %)
British Guiana	9,784	2,019 (20%)
Trinidad	11,506	1,869 (16%)
Jamaica	2,832	237 (8%)
Fiji	10,181	2,091 (20%)
Mauritius	47,000	1,492 (3%)

Disaffection among both indentured and unindentured Indians produced intermittent violence representing one pole on the range of Indian assertiveness; their disaffection created the germ for political activism. In 1872, low wages at Plantation Devonshire Castle produced mass protests where police shot and killed five and wounded seven workers. The *Parliamentary Papers, No. 49* of 1873 claimed that Oederman, a Brahmin (upper caste), was the instigator of this uprising. Planters believed that upper-caste Indians were the source of constant instigations on the estates. The Sugar Planters' Association even urged immigration authorities in Calcutta in 1889 not to recruit upper-caste Indians; and Alleyne Ireland, an overseer, referred to these upper castes as '. . . incorrigible rascals, sowing the seeds of discontent. . . . '

Rigid labor laws produced criminal convictions for the slightest violations. Medical doctors and magistrates operated in the ruling class interests, once they were paid off handsomely. Indian women became frequent targets for sexual assaults by White overseers. Although arrests were common, Indians continued to resist. There was the case in January 1882 of Narain Singh[7] who went to the Immigration Agent-General (IAG) to lodge a complaint pertaining to his wages; he was advised to present his complaint to a magistrate; this he did and the magistrate then invited the manager of Plantation Providence to review Narain Singh's complaint. The manager summoned Narain Singh and told him he was under an indenture contract and that he left the job to proceed to the Immigration- Agent General (IAG) without appropriate permission; the magistrate then dismissed the case.

Gooljar, a returnee, was the chief architect of the 1896 Non Pariel riots. Gooljar came under indenture in 1871, completed his indenture, became a cloth seller, and worked with the police force. He took advantage of the return fare to India in 1890, but returned to Guyana in 1894 as a reindenture. Planters having already had their share of upper caste as instigators, now faced another type of recalcitrant, the reindentured; planters were reluctant to employ renidentureds, as these reindentureds already experienced and expressed bitterness for the 'exploitative' dynamics at play in plantation labor; making them even more motivated to advancing the resistance effort. Bechu, a Bengali immigrant, accorded upper-caste status by planters, was indentured to Plantation Enmore in 1894, but emancipated himself from indentureship in 1897. Bechu aggressively articulated the abuses of indentureship; in November 1896, in penning his first among many letters to the newspaper, Bechu spoke about White overseers' sexual exploitation of Indian females; refusal of estate hospitals to provide medical treatment to unindentured Indians; blatant encouragement of Indians to remain in Guyana, although they eagerly wanted to return to India; and planters' frequent breaches of labor laws pointedly intended to exert total control of Indians. It is remarkable that Bechu was the first Indian to present evidence to a Royal Commission, the West India Royal Commission in 1897. Time-expired (free) Indian immigrants as Gooljar and Bechu, were those most likely to advance the resistance effort; on the other hand, newly-arrived immigrants, the indentureds, were perceived as very malleable. And planters sustained their malleability through a policy that intentionally separated them from free Indians. This 'schism' policy served to reduce free Indian resistance efforts whenever there was a large influx of new immigrants as between 1877 and 1881.

Planters also eliminated any form of organized labor through fragmenting local leadership with transfers to other plantations. For instance, after the 1896 Non Pariel riots, the deputy manager informed the local immigration sub-agent of some small disgruntlement on the plantation, and requested that five immigrants be transferred; they then found their way to Georgetown. Notwithstanding the debilitating capacity of the political struggle under these circumstances, resistance persisted; by the end of the 19th century, Indian resistance definitively began to undermine the power of the plantocracy.

Indian women, too, intensely suffered under indentureship; as victims of abuses, they sparked off protests and so too contributed to the resistance effort as their men folk. Sporadic protests emanated from the weeding gang, largely the women's domain. Salamea, an indentured woman worker was the ringleader of a major disorder at Plantation Friends in Berbice in 1903.[8] Other cases of women's role in the resistance effort abound. Interestingly, Indian worker resistance transcended gender, accelerated the resistance pace through this gender unification, rapidly limiting the planters' monopolistic power, and casting the foundations for middle-class development.

At the turn of the century, middle-class Indians, mainly second-generation attorneys-at-law bonded with working-class and peasant Indians in the struggle for improved education, more fruitful usage of agricultural lands, and better environmental health facilities; a manifestation of intra-ethnic class solidarity; this solidarity within Indian village settlements promoted the welfare of Indians and simultaneously gave credence to the persisting resistance effort. Parahoo, a prominent cattle owner and butcher in Berbice actively supported the welfare of his Muslim brothers and sisters; large Hindu landowners also in like manner advanced the welfare of Hindus; and educated Indians in the IAG lent considerable support to their fellow Indians during indentureship. This thing about promoting welfare might not have been what it seemed to suggest; it was the middle-class way of fortifying its material base. Middle-class Indians exploited other Indians in land purchases and rentals; For instance, Rumburran and Gundoora,[9] purchased seven estates in Berbice; then sold some of the front lands making over 100 percent profit; they rented the backlands at $2.88 per half-acre plot. These were only two cases among many.

A class is only as strong as its material base, meaning that a middle class defined by its fragility and infantilism, would be motivated to reinforce its material base to sustain its dominance; and if this meant exploiting its own ethnic group, so be it. This middle class had control over the means of mental production, so that the working people who lacked the means of mental production became subject to it. Similarly, African and Portuguese proprietors also extended welfare to their respective ethnic groups, and utilized similar dynamics of exploitation.

Unmistakably, in the last quarter of the 19th century, Indian workers and peasants initiated an active resistance effort that was not matched by the emerging local professional Indian middle class; this middle class was urban-based and socialized to accept planters' values; they easily complied with the plantocracy's norms; a behavior quite distinct from the behavior of rural Indian workers and peasants. The Indian middle class tried their hand at establishing the 'East Indian Institute' in 1892, in order to forge enhanced ties with each other, and to be increasingly supportive of the colonial ruling class; it died a natural death; for good reasons, too; for some alignment of this urban Indian middle class with planters implied some disavowal of rural Indian working people's concerns. But the educated Indian middle class became the chief beneficiaries of the emerging political opportunities. Let's look at a laundry list of the colonial and fragile Indian middle class political maneuverings:

Ramdeal was the first Indian to win a seat in 1892 in the Cumberland District of Berbice.

1. Phillip Daniel Guyadeen in 1908 sought a seat in the Combined Court and lost.

2. Prabhu Sawh, an affluent storekeeper in Georgetown unsuccessfully sought permission to place Indians on the official electors' list, as only 0.6% of Indian males from a total of 51.8% of adult Indian males were included in the electoral list in 1911.

3. An Indian was appointed a member of the local authority of the Sheet Anchor County District.

4. Edward Luckhoo, a solicitor, elected Mayor of New Amsterdam.

5. Indians fully represented in local authority districts in the villages founded by Indians and those set up by the Government in lieu of a return passage to India.

6. Indians approved a Resolution of Dissociation against the recall of Governor Egerton by Africans and Colored groups.

7. The British Guiana East Indian Association (BGEIA) established in 1916 had no mass following; it functioned within the middle-class and not the working people's interests.

C.R. Jacob was elected to the Legislative Council in 1935; and Ayube Edun was nominated to that Council in 1943. Both organized the Manpower Citizens'

Association in 1936. They addressed working people's issues, but had no mass following; with no mass foundation, there was indeed political vacuum, as workers' issues were largely unresolved.

Dr. Cheddi Jagan assessed this political scene in the 1940s; he saw planters and the political middle class were only interested in preserving the status quo; there was no mass-based party; and the working people's interests and needs were excluded from both the Indian and African middle-class agenda. Dr. Jagan with Ashton Chase, Jocelyn Hubbard, and his wife Janet Jagan, then sought to fill this vacuum, bringing forth a new dawn in Guyana's politics; the Political Affairs Committee (PAC), forerunner to the People's Progressive Party (PPP), heralding the beginnings of the mass-based party and the articulation and resolution of workers' concerns.

The PPP continued from where the PAC left off; unrelenting agitation for Independence became the number one item on the PPP's agenda. This feverish campaigning prompted the arrival of the Waddington Commission; this was a success long in the making for the PPP struggle against colonial hegemony; a struggle that conceived and gave birth to universal adult suffrage; a struggle that designed the road map for Independence. The first election under universal adult suffrage happened in 1953 during the Cold War.

In the run-up to the 1953 election, Daniel Debidin, a Solicitor, was Leader of the United Farmers' and Workers' Party; earlier, he defeated John Carter to enter the Legislative Council in 1947; Debidin's subsequently party evicted itself from the electoral contest and he ran as an Independent, obtaining 16.7% of electoral votes. Debidin's problem was that his political vision focused only on middle-class Indians and not on working-class people in this multiethnic society. Another middle-class Indian Dr. J.B. Singh who was in the Legislative Council for 21 years, contested the 1953 election. PPP's Fred Bowman (with 42.3% of the votes) defeated Dr. Singh (with 26% of the votes) in an Indian-dominated constituency. General Secretary of the Man Power Citizens' Association (MPCA) Sheik M. Shakoor lost his deposit securing only 411 votes. Balram Singh Rai, an Attorney-at-Law, was a National Democratic Party (NDP) candidate for the Central Demerara constituency in 1953; he lost his deposit securing only 421 votes. Rai became a member of the PPP after the suspension of the constitution in 1953.

The PPP won in 1953 bringing forth the first national unity government in Guyana that included Dr. J.P. Lachhmansingh and Jai Narine Singh as Ministers; the latter lost his election bid to the Legislative Council in 1947 and became a member of the PPP just before the 1953 election. After the PPP's removal from office in 1953, Jai Narine Singh, among others, engineered the PPP split in 1955.

The colonial authorities constituted the interim government of the 1954-1957 years with mainly anti-PPP people from the middle class and elite groupings comprising such Indians as Rahaman Gajraj, James Ramphal, and Lionel Luckhoo, among others

There were many stalwarts like Ram Karran and several Africans like Ashton Chase who remained loyal to Jagan's PPP. Ram Karran was with the PPP from the 1950s, becoming a Minister in the 1957 PPP Government that also included Edward Beharry; Beharry's position was later rescinded in 1960 due to his anti-government position on the tax measures concerning the sugar industry. The PPP won the elections again in 1961. And its 1962 budget drew the ire of wealthy Indians, many of whom joined the United Force, such as Rahaman Gajraj, and Hari Prashad who became its Chairman. At this time, several well-known Indians opposed the PPP; these included Balwant Singh, Richard Ishmael, Hoosein Ganie, Abdool Majeed, an affluent Indian merchant and President of the United Sad'r Islamic Anjuman.

Rai was no longer a PPP member by the time of the 1964 elections. His Justice Party (JP) secured a mere 1,334 votes; and Hoosein Ganie's Guyana United Muslim Party (GUMP) obtained 1,194 votes. Rai called for Indian votes on the grounds that the PPP was anti-Indian and anti-religious; one of Ganie's handbills told the Guyanese people that "A vote for GUMP was a vote for Allah'. Guyana's electoral history pointedly indicates that political leaders only focusing on their own class interests reinforced with blatant opportunism, and not the people's interests, falter at electoral times. Then there is Reepu Daman Persaud, a product of plantation labor, a PPP Member of Parliament for 40 years and founder of the Guyana Hindu Dharmic Sabha; he currently holds the portfolio of Minister of Parliamentary Affairs; acted as Prime Minister and as President of Guyana on several occasions.

Clearly, Indians were not docile during indentureship. Indians demonstrated a remarkable history of active resistance. Labor unrest that facilitated Indian solidarity also simultaneously was a remarkable method used for ensuring cultural persistence. The dynamic resistance to achieve and sustain cultural persistence and continuity created the ingredients for an Indian political evolution and mobilization. Indentured Indian working people, through their challenge to colonial hegemony, created the Indian political middle class; but that early political middle class idolized colonialism inimical to workers' concerns; the later political middle class steeped in advancing its own ethnic group's interests, blatant opportunism, and imperialist intrigue, also neglected workers' concerns. The Indian political middle class has not delivered the goods; time for recreation of a new Indian middle class, to work in solidarity with Indian workers, and eventually reaching out to the working people of this country in sustainable alliances.

Notes

1. Tinker, Hugh. *A New System of Slavery: The Export of Indian Labor Overseas, 1830-1920*. Oxford, 1974.
2. Nath, Dwarka. *A History of Indians in British Guiana*. London, 1950, p. 16.

3. Jayawardena, Chandra. *Conflict and Solidarity on a Guianese Planta-tion.* London, 1963, p. 17.
4. Comins, D.W. *Note on Emigration from India to British Guiana.* Cal-cutta, 1893, p. 96.
5. Ireland, W. Alleyne. *Demerariana.* Georgetown, 1897.
6. *The Sanderson Commission.* Parliamentary Papers. 27, 1910, p. 13.
7. Court of Review, 1882.
8. Guyana National Archives., GD 190, May 20, 1903.
9. Report on Commission of Back Passages, 1895.

Shaping Indian Politics through Worker Resistance Part 3

In Part 1 of this series on Indian resistance, I spoke about African resistance as strategic to the abolition of slavery; planters' goal of wanting total control of labor after slavery; Indian labor fitting the planters' 'total control' framework in early recruitment; indentureship, a new system of slavery; Indians in a dehuman-ized total institutional environment; Indian arrivals as outsiders then and as 'out-siders' even today; and the beginnings of Indian resistance.

Part 2 illustrated the role of Oederman, Narain Singh, Bechu, Gooljar, Salamea, and Parahoo in adding intensity to the Indian resistance; and the birth of the Indian middle class showing early signs of its capacity to exploit fellow Indians, as exemplified through Rumburran and Gundoora of the Berbice es-tates.

Workers through active struggle cemented the foundations for Indian politi-cal evolution in this country; the Indian middle class political role was egocen-tric, substandard, exploitative, albeit that they were the chief beneficiaries of workers' efforts. Let's further explore this line of thinking.

Unmistakably, in the last quarter of the 19th century, Indian workers and peasants initiated an active resistance effort that was not matched by the emerg-ing local professional Indian middle class; this middle class was urban-based and socialized to accept planters' values; they easily complied with the plan-tocracy's norms; a behavior quite distinct from the behavior of rural Indian workers and peasants.

The Indian middle class tried their hand at establishing the 'East Indian In-stitute' in 1892, in order to forge enhanced ties with each other, and to be in-creasingly supportive of the colonial ruling class; it died a natural death; for good reasons, too; for some alignment of this urban Indian middle class with planters implied some disavowal of rural Indian working people's concerns.

But this educated Indian middle class became the chief beneficiaries of the emerging political opportunities. Let's look at a laundry list of the colonialist-oriented and fragile Indian middle class political maneuverings:

1. Ramdeal was the first Indian to win a seat in 1892 in the Cumberland District of Berbice.
2. Phillip Daniel Guyadeen in 1908 sought a seat in the Combined Court and lost.
3. Prabhu Sawh, an affluent storekeeper in Georgetown unsuccessfully sought permission to place Indians on the official electors' list, as only 0.6% of Indian males from a total of 51.8% of adult Indian males were included in the electoral list in 1911.
4. An Indian was appointed a member of the local authority of the Sheet Anchor County District.
5. Edward Luckhoo, a solicitor, elected Mayor of New Amsterdam.
6. Indians fully represented in local authority districts in villages founded by Indians and those set up by the Government in lieu of a return passage to India.
7. Indians approved a Resolution of Dissociation against the recall of Governor Egerton by Africans and Colored groups.
8. The British Guiana East Indian Association (BGEIA) established in 1916 had no mass following; it functioned within the middle-class and not the working people's interests.
9. C.R. Jacob was elected to the Legislative Council in 1935; and Ayube Edun was nominated to that Council in 1943. Both organized the Manpower Citizens' Association in 1936. They addressed working people's issues, but had no mass following; with no mass foundation, there was indeed political vacuum, as workers' issues were largely unresolved.

Dr. Cheddi Jagan assessed this political scene in the 1940s; he saw planters and the political middle class were only interested in preserving the status quo; there was no mass-based party; and the working people's interests and needs were excluded from both the Indian and African middle-class agenda. Dr. Jagan with Ashton Chase, Jocelyn Hubbard, and his wife Janet Jagan, then sought to fill this vacuum, bringing forth a new dawn in Guyana's politics: the creation of the Political Affairs Committee (PAC), forerunner to the People's Progressive Party (PPP), heralding the beginnings of the mass-based party and the articulation and resolution of workers' concerns.

The PPP continued from where the PAC left off; unrelenting agitation for Independence became the number one item on the PPP's agenda. This feverish campaigning prompted the arrival of the Waddington Commission; this was a success long in the making for the PPP struggle against colonial hegemony; a struggle that conceived and gave birth to universal adult suffrage; a struggle that designed the road map for Independence. Then came the first election under universal adult suffrage in 1953 during the Cold War.

In the run-up to the 1953 election, Daniel Debidin, a Solicitor, was Leader of the United Farmers' and Workers' Party; earlier, he defeated John Carter to enter the Legislative Council in 1947; Debidin's party subsequently evicted it-self from the 1953 electoral contest and he ran as an Independent, obtaining 16.7% of electoral votes. Debidin's problem was that his political vision focused only on middle-class Indians and not on working-class people in this multiethnic society.

Another middle-class Indian Dr. J.B. Singh who was in the Legislative Council for 21 years, contested the 1953 election. PPP's Fred Bowman (with 42.3% of the votes) defeated Dr. Singh (with 26% of the votes) in an Indian-dominated constituency. General Secretary of the Man Power Citizens' Association (MPCA) Sheik M. Shakoor lost his deposit accruing only 411 votes. Balram Singh Rai, an Attorney-at-Law, was a National Democratic Party (NDP) candidate for the Central Demerara constituency in 1953; he lost his deposit securing only 421 votes. Rai became a member of the PPP after the suspension of the Constitution in 1953.

The PPP won in 1953 bringing forth the first national unity government in Guyana that included Ashton Chase, Forbes Burnham, Dr. J.P. Lachhmansingh, and Jai Narine Singh as Ministers; Jai Narine Singh lost his election bid to the Legislative Council in 1947 and became a member of the PPP just before the 1953 election. After the PPP's removal from office in 1953, Jai Narine Singh, among others, engineered the PPP split in 1955.

The colonial authorities constituted the interim government of the 1954-1957 years with mainly anti-PPP people from the middle class and elite group-ings, comprising such Indians as Rahaman Gajraj, James Ramphal, and Lionel Luckhoo, among others

There were many stalwarts like Ram Karran and several Africans like Ashton Chase who remained loyal to Jagan's PPP. Ram Karran was with the PPP from the 1950s, becoming a Minister in the 1957 PPP Government that also included Edward Beharry; Beharry's position was later rescinded in 1960 due to his anti-government position on the tax measures concerning the sugar industry.

The PPP won the elections again in 1961. And its 1962 budget drew the ire of wealthy Indians, many of whom joined the United Force, such as Rahaman Gajraj, and Hari Prashad who became its Chairman. At this time, several well-known Indians opposed the PPP; these included Balwant Singh, Richard Ish-mael, Hoosein Ganie, Abdool Majeed, an affluent Indian merchant and Presi-dent of the United Sad'r Islamic Anjuman.

Rai was no longer a PPP member by the time of the 1964 elections. His Jus-tice Party (JP) secured a mere 1,334 votes; and Hoosein Ganie's Guyana United Muslim Party (GUMP) obtained 1,194 votes. Rai called for Indian votes on the grounds that the PPP was anti-Indian and anti-religious; one of Ganie's hand-bills told the Guyanese people that "A vote for GUMP was a vote for Allah'.

Then there is Reepu Daman Persaud, a product of plantation labor, a PPP Member of Parliament for 40 years and founder of the Guyana Hindu Dharmic Sabha; he currently holds the portfolio of Minister of Parliamentary Affairs; acted as Prime Minister and as President of Guyana on several occasions. He has mastered the art of effectively mixing his Hindu priestly functions with politics.

Guyana's electoral history pointedly indicates that political leaders only focusing on their own class interests partnered with blatant opportunism, and not the people's interests, would falter at electoral times.

Clearly, Indians were not docile during indentureship. Indians demonstrated a remarkable history of active resistance. Labor unrest that facilitated Indian solidarity also simultaneously was a striking method used for ensuring cultural persistence. The dynamic resistance to achieve and sustain cultural persistence and continuity created the ingredients for Indian political evolution and mobilization.

Indentured Indian working people, through their challenge to colonial hegemony, created the Indian political middle class; but that early political middle class idolized colonialism, inimical to workers' concerns; the later political middle class steeped in advancing its own ethnic group's interests at the expense of others', blatant opportunism, and imperialist intrigue, also neglected workers' concerns.

The Indian political middle class has not delivered the goods; time for re-creation of a new Indian middle class, to work in solidarity with Indian workers, and to reach out to the working people of this country in sustainable alliances.

Guyana not Ridden with Racial & Ethnic Conflict

Many multiethnic societies have a dominant group followed by several subordinate groups, producing some form of ethnic stratification. And, indeed, the dominant ethnic group has total access to the valued resources of society, with subordinate groups picking up only subsistence rewards. The dominant ethnic group, generally, sustains its control, power, and privileges through prejudice and discrimination. Prejudice can be seen as a judgment "based on a fixed mental image of some group or class of people and applied to all individuals of that class without being tested against reality" (Mason, 1970). In fact ethnic prejudices are generalized, inflexible, negative, and are based on erroneous group images known as stereotypes. Discrimination, on the other hand, is a behavior denying opportunities and equal rights to individuals and groups due to prejudice or for other capricious reasons. In effect, prejudice is attitudinal while discrimination is behavioral.

Guyana, as a multiethnic society, does not have a singular dominant ethnic group, as evidenced through access to education and jobs by all ethnics. Spectacular education outcomes and high-level jobs are in the hands of all ethnic groups. We do not see, for instance, only East Indians, or only Africans excelling at CXC and SSEE. And, indeed, unemployment and poverty do not plague only one ethnic group. In some multiethnic societies in the developing world, we can observe a rigid ethnic stratification with the impressive education outcomes and jobs going mainly to the dominant ethnic group. Where there is rigid ethnic stratification, there are the accompanying forms of prejudice and discrimination.

Guyana does not have a rigid ethnic stratification system. Given this situation, many aspects of this country's racial and ethnic conflict are politically and socially constructed and reconstructed by ethnic leaders jockeying for political power. In Guyana, daily, we see the cynical manipulation by ethnic leaders or shall I say, so-called ethnic leaders, whose main agenda is penetrating the backdoor entrance to political power. It, therefore, is in these ethnic leaders' interests to keep ethnic and racial conflicts alive.

We need to remind ourselves that Guyanese history is not inundated with racial conflict but ethnic alliances. However, some politicians want us to believe that racial and ethnic conflict is endemic in this society. Rodney makes the point that the case advanced of highly prevalent racial conflict in the society is inaccurate. This is what he has to say:

> . . . my contention is that the case for the dominant role of racial division in the historical sphere has been overstated, and that scholarship on the subject has accepted without due scrutiny the proposition that Indians and Africans existed in mutually exclusive compartments. The problems of interpretation lie not only in the marshalling of the evidence, but, more fundamentally, in the historical methodology that is applied (Rodney 1982:188).

Let us now look at a few facts supporting this notion that Guyana's history is not ridden with racial and ethnic conflict.

- The Commonwealth Commission commenting on the disturbances in 1962: "We found little evidence of any racial segregation in the social life of the country...East Indians and Africans seemed to mix and associate with one another on terms of the greatest cordiality. . . ."
- There is the alliance between East Indians and Africans under Critchlow's leadership in the fight for better wages, and an 8-hour working day.
- The union of ethnic forces against colonial hegemony is another case in point, e.g., the frequent criticisms launched by the Indian Opinion, the organ of the British Guiana East Indian Association, against the colonial government; Africans challenging the anti-education principles of the 1876 Education law; the demand for Indian languages to be introduced in schools; and the Court of Policy comprising members from many ethnic groups made crown lands available to both East Indians and Africans.
- The emergence of institutional working-class unity in 1946 that became solidified in 1950 with the formation of the People's Progressive Party and the unity manifested by its victory at the 1953 polls.
- H.J.M. Hubbard, a trade unionist in addressing whether Guyana is ridden with racial conflict said:

It is by any standards a remarkable fact that in a competitive semi-feudal society such as British Guiana with restricted social and economic opportunities and less jobs than potential workers, very few serious physical inter-racial conflicts arose between the ethnic groups constituting the population (Hubbard 1969:27).

Political Deception

The threshold of the White colonialists' departure from the Colonies, that is, from the 1950s to the present, saw ethnic competition between the major ethnic groups to fill the power vacuum and secure the legal-political stage. The ethnic division arising out of this ethnic competition was intentional and a subterfuge used by some politicians to secure political advantage along ethnic lines. That is, it is an invented racial antagonism not rooted in sustained racial and ethnic hatred, but political deceit.

This deception and pretense whereby racial conflict is presented as afflicting the total society, has had its institutional origins in the early 1950s. The split within the PPP in 1955 struck a blow to East Indian and African working-class unity. The unity became further strained following the People's National Congress (PNC) electoral loss in 1957.

Dr. Jagan in his West On Trial earmarked the PNC's defeat in 1957 as the beginning of racial party politics. At that time, according to Jagan, Burnham allied himself with the United Democratic Party's leadership comprising John Carter and Rudy Kendall who were connected to the African racist League of Colored People. Further defeat of the PNC in the 1961 election drove that Party more intensively toward African racism. Jagan noted:

> In New York City and in the UN corridors, American Blacks and African diplomats were told that the PPP government was penalizing the Africans. At home, African workers were told that the Indians owned the lands and the big houses in Georgetown, were taking over Water Street (the commercial center), and that if they (the Africans) were not careful, the Indians would soon take over their jobs (Jagan 1997:301).

There are numerous examples of political deception camouflaged as ethnic conflict or engineering this ethnic conflict, evidenced by the daily adumbration through the broadcast media.

The history of Guyana does not support a high prevalence of ethnic conflict and violence, as evidenced in some multiethnic societies steeped in prejudice, discrimination, and segregation. Today, the principles of divisive ethnic rules, as used in colonialism, are again applied today for capturing the prized legal-political stage that is the government and state.

Fueling Ethnic Conflict & Polarization: Ordinary Guyanese People not Guilty

In Guyana, all confrontations are explained through ethnic conflicts. Indeed, some conflicts are related to ethnic or cultural identity. But most of these conflicts have nothing to do with ethnicity; most have to do with some people wanting to acquire political power or other resources.

In Guyana, some politicians, private media, and now architects of hate literature, fuel ethnic conflict and violence as well as ethnic polarization. The ordinary people are not guilty of this ideational carnage.

But this group's brutal quest to secure political power requires planting seeds of racial discord, to falsely demonstrate that the African group is shortchanged. Their solution to eliminating this shortchanging is to put in place shared governance. We already have an evolving system of political inclusivity or shared governance. Their view, albeit false, is that lack of shared governance is a catalyst for conflict and underperformance of the economy.

Again, I want to suggest that this group's mistaken view of ethnic marginalization (see Misir, 2002), a failed economy, and lack of inclusivity, is not supported by the evidence. This group intentionally misrepresents the genesis of conflict to achieve its own political agenda, as the roots of the Guyana conflict reside not in primordial ethnic differences, but in a group of people attempting to secure power and other resources using the race card.

The economy in is not in shambles, despite shortfalls in sugar and gold production. In 2003, the value of sugar exported rose by 8.1%. Rice, livestock, forestry, and services showed increases in general performance. The volume of rice exported increased by 4%. Export receipts for bauxite increased to US$44.6 million. Merchandise exports were US$517 million, 4.3% more than 2002.

Liquidity growth was controlled impacting inflation at 4.9% and exchange rate contained at G$194.25 per US dollar. The new minimum wage ($22,099) plus income tax threshold increase plus containing inflation produced an increased disposable income. Current revenue for central government was $45.4 billion, a 1.8% improvement on 2002.

Sometimes we focus excessively on how much the GDP per capita, that is, the average production of the country's people, increased. But we need to address other factors, too, such as, how evenly economic benefits are distributed, the condition of the environment, and people's health status.

It is insufficient to inquire as to whether people are prospering. Instead, a better question is: how fully are people living? The Human Development Index provides better information on a nation's people than GDP. The Human Development Index combines indicators of GDP per capita, life expectancy, and education, into one index score. Guyana has shown progress on the Human Development Index, as reported in the last UNDP's Human Development Report.

Inclusive Governance

President Bharrat Jagdeo presented the PPP/C's position on inclusive governance in 2003 at the State House. The paper came at a time when everybody seems to have an opinion on shared governance. However, the President's paper, true to form, sustains a long established tradition where the PPP has always advocated constitutional reforms to enhance the governance process and promoting national unity. National unity in a multi-ethnic society must be a strategic goal of any governance process, and as far back as 1965, we observe Cheddi Jagan's call for racial harmony.

President Bharrat Jagdeo and then Leader of the Opposition PNCR the late Mr. Hugh Desmond Hoyte in 2001 established an inter-party committee system that yielded enormous benefits to the people.

Constitutional amendments, and we have quite a few, are a significant form of an evolving culture of inclusiveness. However, the PNCR's absence from Parliament retards the social growth of these amendments.

The opposition has a useful contributory role in enhancing the governance process mainly through the parliamentary committee systems, questions, and motions in Parliament it does not constitutionally perform the functions of government. Any opposition party's role in a parliamentary democracy and the existing parliamentary committee system already are an exercise in an evolving inclusiveness.

We need to embrace the evolving structures of parliamentary inclusiveness that we have, instead of latching on to an executive power sharing model that lacks the capability to (1) address change, (2) institutionalize racial and ethnic competition, (3) influence the absence of an opposition, and (4) exclude the role of the masses in decision making. Executive power sharing has had limited success around the world, as in Northern Ireland, Ivory Coast, etc.

However, whatever change we introduce requires trust, a precondition for real success. Trust is an emotional skill that we construct and sustain with our promises and commitments, our emotions and integrity. We need to build not an immature trust that is effortlessly shattered, but an authentic trust that is time-honored, reflective, and renewable. Trust is necessary for good governance which starts with the existing structures of parliamentary inclusiveness. What we do not need is a false trust that politically manipulates the race card.

Toward Pluralist Unity in Multicultural Societies

Good governance in multiracial societies generally ensures the confluence of each ethnic group's culture to create national unity. National unity must not mean a dilution of the ethnics' cultures. National unity must mean pluralist unity where there is a dynamic coexistence of each group's culture. National unity must create space and appreciation for all cultures. National unity must not mean giving a higher status to some cultures to the exclusion of other cultures. Ethnics should be given space to unite within a mosaic of all cultures. This institutional mosaic will be the truest manifestation of national unity. All cultures must be on a level playing field.

For the moment, however, some forces, though well-intentioned, are diligently at work to spread the gospel of national unity that somehow in theory will be devoid of the cultural presence of all ethnic groups. These forces see national unity as requiring something unique and separate from the existing cultural life of the society. Apparently, these advocates for national unity believe that such unity will be clothed in a brand new culture quite different from the existing cultural mosaic. This kind of advocacy is a recipe for national disintegration.

In fact, this 'E Pluribus Unum' (out of many, one) approach to national unity reminds me of the 'melting pot' concept in the U.S. The melting pot theory in the U.S. posits that all the nationalities eventually would blend into one 'American' culture. This method requires that the society builds a new and distinctive culture from the diverse experiences of its ethnics. In the U.S., the first President George Washington believed in the melting pot theory whereby future immigrants would become 'one people'. This process failed. What eventually happened was that the cultures did not melt but persisted into a hierarchy of ethnic cultures. Then and even today in the U.S., despite the advent of multiculturalism, Eurocentrism dominates.

Any ethnic hierarchy creates a process of subordination and superordination, so much so that some cultures are favored and others are not. These conditions, inevitably, will produce ethnic cleavage and closure. Cleavage eventually will produce dysfunctional consequences, unless some dominant group takes control over all ethnic enclaves. Eurocentrism has accomplished just that in the U.S. However, there is the argument that in the U.S., Eurocentrism was always present, but with the enduring belief that all the cultural experiences would evaporate into one culture. What did not occur was a 'cultural meltdown'. Instead, we saw the growth of an ethnic hierarchy in the U.S., with Eurocentrism being the dominant cultural pattern. There are important lessons here for developing multicultural societies, in terms of how not to create a national culture and national unity. No national unity must be birthed from cultural meltdown and/or ethnic dominance. A particular perspective, the plural theory, has advanced the notion that national integration requires the presence of a dominant group amid a sleigh of ethnic enclaves; the alternative, according to this theory, is national disintegration.

The problem that ensues is that ethnic dominance not only supports an ethnic hierarchy, but works toward diluting the cultural patterns of ethnics, in the quest for achieving national unity. Smith (1965:82), a plural theorist, saw each ethnic group in society as self-sustaining ethnic enclaves for its members. This plural society, Smith contended, had no common value system. The absence of a common belief system demonstrated the need for controlling the overall social order; the dominant cultural community, therefore, maintained order. However, Smith believed that the subordinate cultural segments did not wholly depend on the dominant ethnic group, since they developed their own social structure that was invariably in conflict with the dominant group thereby reinforcing the need for ethnic dominance.

Smith, nevertheless, may have overestimated the role of different cultural communities, by excluding class in the analysis. Excluding class enabled Smith to show practically no meaningful social interaction among the ethnic communities. But each community had a stratification system based not only on race and ethnicity, but on class, too. Both African and East Indian communities were comprised of upper, middle, and lower classes. A lower-class East Indian was more inclined to interact with a lower-class African as well as with other lower-class East Indians than with Africans and East Indians of the upper classes, and vice versa. Interaction only occurring within a particular class is a manifestation of class cleavage which is highly characteristic of the following two situations: The situation where East Indians only interacted with other East Indians of the same class, is referred to as intra-ethnic class cleavage. The situation where East Indians and Africans of the same class only interacted with other East Indians and Africans of the same class, can be called inter-ethnic class cleavage. These inter-ethnic class interactions, at any rate, show a closely-wedded structure among Smith's ethnic enclaves, contrary to what he presented.

Races 'coming together'
However, people who constantly talk about the need for races to 'come together', lack a basic understanding of the power dynamics of race and ethnic relations in a multiethnic society 'coming together' is invariably intended to mean the development of national unity in developing societies where only some cultures are allowed seating at the head table. That is, where ethnic hierarchy and dominance exists. The cultures of the masses, in this context, are excluded and are reduced to a subordinate status.

The Spanish writer Ortega Y Gasset who authored INVERTEBRATE SPAIN, aptly explains the process that keeps a multiethnic group of people together, thus "People don't live together just like that. That kind of cohesion exists only within a family. The groups who make up a state live together for a purpose. They are a community of projects, desires, big undertakings. They don't come together simply to be together, but in order to do something tomorrow." Ortego's cohesion is not achieved because the minority people's cultures are underemphasized.

Naipaul in a keynote speech at a conference held at the University of the West Indies, St. Augustine, tried to paint a picture of the impact of the colonial attitude. His position on how diversified groups of people come together, supports that of Ortego. Naipaul drew attention to a European colonial administrator who complained about why the local people did not come together.

He criticizes this colonialist's cognitive process that sees the local peoples as having no distinctive qualities, and that all of them can be compartmentalized into one cultural non-distinguishing brownish mass. Naipaul rejects this colonialist's assertion as "It concedes humanity, it concedes a past, a particularity, and a pride, only to one particular group. It concedes these things only to one people— the administrator's people — and it denies them to everyone else."

The European colonialist's conception of national unity was the compartmentalization of all the locals into one cultural group, resocializing them to show deference to Anglo-culture and to subscribe to Anglo-conformity. This colonialist's thinking and action amount to cultural imperialism where everything that is 'White' is superior and that whatever is nonwhite is inferior. Naipaul rejects this cultural imperialism.

One People

This scenario is an illustration of assimilation of minorities to a dominant White group's culture. That was the basis of national unity in colonial times. Naipaul was right. But Naipaul went further to say that this colonial conception has persisted. In the case of Trinidad & Tobago (T&T), Naipaul believes that T&T people present to outsiders their picturesqueness, and the cosmopolitan population at a trivial level. In other words, they use tourist concepts to introduce their society. Such tourist concepts solidify simplicities and ignorance about diversified people's history and achievements. We do this because we have been socialized and re-socialized by the colonialists to accept that the many different local people are really one people. This situation applies to Guyana, too. But the people of Guyana, T&T, and other developing multicultural societies, have varied cultural patterns. They certainly are not one people. They are different, as they have different cultures.

If we accept this position of being one people, and as such, having achieved national unity, then we are acknowledging cultural loss to each ethnic minority group. We are admitting to the society being a cemetery of cultures. If you doubt this, look at the impact of cultural imperialism in education and politics in the Caribbean. This overwhelming aura of the colonialists' conception of national unity, seeing all locals as one people has reached maturation in the Caribbean, as we continue to use the colonialists' rules.

Avoiding a Cultural Irrationality

Politicians thought that use of the term 'Guyanese culture' and baptizing everybody as having a 'Guyanese culture' would heal all and eliminate the deformities of the society. Using the term 'Guyanese culture' is just like an admission of the cultural non-distinctiveness of all the peoples of Guyana. The cultural content and parameters of the application of the term 'Guyanese culture' is fully controlled by the dominant group. This is so because the cultural capital of Guyana is owned and controlled by the group that wields considerable economic and political power. Naipaul would say that it is disheartening to think that these attitudes, such as using the term 'Guyanese culture', which at first might seem revolutionary, is really the other side of the old colonial attitudes. He said "What looks new is only a reaction to the old, is conditioned by the old. I think this is the kind of irrationality that we must avoid."

Let all people in Guyana do some self-examination of links to their cultural heritage. This process involves going beyond the boundaries of slavery and indentureship. We must connect to our roots. In the United States, no credence is given to unifying all the people's cultures in the society. Attempts in Guyana through the National Service were previously made to effect this goal. The policy failed. Such cultural unification in the U.S., if it becomes a reality, would still be subordinated to the power elite. This would be assimilation to Anglo-conformity which is highly irrelevant and unnecessary. In the U.S., pluralism, implying the coexistence and acceptance of each ethnic group's culture is in vogue, and is characterized by an element of permanence. People in the U.S. together engage in projects and work collectively, against a background of institutional recognition of each ethnic group's culture.

Pluralist Unity

Pluralism and multiculturalism are the most logical, secure, and enterprising form of national unity in a multiethnic society. To be a 'Guyanese', is to accept and celebrate the diversity of ethnic cultures in Guyana. This is the kind of persisting national unity that Guyanese want and deserve.' Guyanese culture' must not be applied to mean merely one culture; there is not one Guyanese culture, but many Guyanese cultures.

Guyana can enhance race and ethnic relations by eliminating the term 'national unity' grounded in this thing called 'Guyanese culture', from the political lexicon. In theory, 'national unity' implies the presence of an elite determining the parameters of societal unification, and hegemony over other ethnic groups in the society. This type of national unity trapped in a 'Guyanese culture' is not feasible, and is antagonistic to cultural diversity.

But Guyana, being highly stratified by class and race, with considerable amounts of inequality, cannot embrace a national unity that excludes pluralism political acknowledgment and institutionalization of each ethnic group's culture will improve race and ethnic relations.

The 'national unity' goal, devoid of a pluralist base in a multiethnic and stratified system, requires as a pre-condition some significant cultural loss to all ethnic groups, but not to the elite. This is so because 'national unity' based on a 'Guyanese culture', as a political expedient and rhetoric, refers to the acceptance of some different and higher values advocated by the elite, and are not part of the minority multiethnic landscape. Generally, the elite's values are contradictory to those of the minority groups.

The elite wants to see the acceptance of these higher values because these values, being treated as having more potency than the minority multicultural values, sustain their vested economic interests.

The 'national unity' goal, under these conditions of excluding the values of minority ethnics, is fertile ground for an emerging community of irrationality. People will not come together in this community of irrationality.

Pluralist unity grounded in an equal status among all ethnic cultures is a more feasible and attractive alternative. If, however, you still are turned on to use the term 'national unity', then that 'national unity' must be grounded in pluralism. 'National unity' must not pander to one ethnic culture, at the exclusion of other minority cultures.

Sometimes we hear the Loudest Yelps for Freedom from the Drivers of Race Hate

Almost every issue in Guyana is explained through racism. This is an error. Why? An issue mistakenly seen as caused by racism may not be adequately resolved because the diagnosis is incorrect. Wrong diagnosis may produce wrong treatment. The culprits who deliberately plug this error are the new political operatives—some 'pure' politicians, private media, and race-hate specialists. The media's operation is presented as cunning biases.

The White colonial planters operating as political operatives applied racism in pursuit of their political and economic ends. Today, the situation is no different. Today's politics have an enduring relationship with racism. But this political terrain is no longer the exclusive preserve of 'pure' politicians. *What must be made explicitly clear is that the people are not guilty of creating this racism.* However, the new political operatives are guilty of peddling this racism to the masses of Guyanese people.

The masses must be educated to know that particular political operatives exploit the race factor to gain electoral advantage. It is this political exploitation that drives racial mistrust and fear. The ethnic polarization is not driven by the masses, but by particular political functionaries, the private media, and race-hate specialists. The large numbers of Guyanese people are not a party to this ensemble of racial agitators masquerading as political operatives.

Why the Rwanda Genocide?

Explanations of the Rwanda genocide in 1994 place the blame fully where it belongs, on politics. Initially, the world was led to believe that tribal hatred between the Hutus and Tutsis caused the genocide.

But the BBC Africa Correspondent explains the genocide, thus:

Like many of my colleagues, I drove into [Rwanda] believing the short stocky ones had simply decided to turn on the tall thin ones because that was the way it has always been. Yet now, two years later . . . I think the answer is very different. What happened in Rwanda was the result of cynical manipulation by powerful political and military leaders. Faced with the choice of sharing some of their wealth and power with the [insurgent] Rwandan Patriotic Front, they chose to vilify that organization's main support group, the Tutsis. . . . The Tutsis were characterized as vermin. Inyenzi in kinyarwanda—cockroaches who should be stamped on without mercy . . . In much the same way as the Nazis exploited latent anti-Semitism in Germany, so did the forces of Hutu extremism identify and whip into murderous frenzy the historical sense of grievance against the Tutsis. . . . This was not about tribalism first and foremost but about preserving the concentration of wealth and power in the hands of the elite.

The process used for concentrating power into a few hands requires political manipulation and all the niceties that go with politics. Also, the media in Rwanda aggressively promoted incitement to genocidal acts, in order to further the goals of wealth concentration. Again, in Rwanda, it was a new group of political operatives, including the media and race-hate specialists that drove the racism and tribal hatred. It's easy to see that the Hutu masses were guilty of executing this genocide; they essentially were a facade for the political operatives' nefarious activities. The Hutu masses were politically manipulated, all in the name of gaining political power. In many ways, the pre-genocidal preparation spawned the destabilization process, leading to the ultimate, 'genocide'.

The Private Media Biases

Many preparatory activities, including misrepresentation of facts and racial incitement, necessary for destabilization, are a hallmark of the new political operatives' behavior in Guyana. Quite recently, the Stabroek News misrepresented an International Monetary Fund (IMF) release to mean that the IMF requires a feasibility study as a pre-condition for construction of the cricket stadium. This is what Stabroek News in a front-page headline captioned 'IMF bowls cricket stadium googly' said:

> The International Monetary Fund (IMF) has asked the government to undertake a feasibility study of the proposed cricket stadium, noting that it should meet certain targets as set out in Guyana's Poverty Reduction and Growth Facility (PRGF)...

This is what the IMF release said:

> To improve the quality and efficiency of public spending and safeguard debt sustainability, the authorities plan to establish a five-year rolling Public Sector Investment Program, to conduct feasibility studies for all large projects, and to strengthen procurement procedures. In this context, the authorities have committed to keep the planned construction of a sports stadium within the program's fiscal, debt, and social spending targets, and to take compensatory measures, if necessary, on the basis of a feasibility study.

The IMF reported in its media release what the Government of Guyana (GoG) intends to do, and what it intends to do, inter alia, includes the conduct of a feasibility study for the cricket stadium. There clearly is no instruction from the IMF to the GoG to administer a feasibility study for the cricket stadium, as suggested by Stabroek News. The GoG also assures the IMF that it intends to keep the construction of the stadium within its proposed Public Sector Investment Program's fiscal, debt, and social expenditure goals.

This is mischievous reporting that is quite consistent with the notion that some private media are engaged as political operatives in frequent aggressive and harmful coverage. In this case, it appears that the media in question has experienced some ecstasy in a possible delay in constructing the stadium. Again, earlier this year, Stabroek News mentioned that George Bacchus was subject to a lie-detector test at the United States Embassy. We later learnt that that was a lie. The Guyanese people need to know about these mischievous media coverage, especially as they are the victims of frequent media biases, sometimes indirectly tinged with racial incitement. This kind of irresponsible reporting promotes the destabilization agenda.

Promoting a Culture of Race Hate

Notwithstanding the daily dosage of media biases and racism aimed at widening ethnic polarization for destabilization purposes, the masses of all ethnic groups are not hateful of each other. The UN Special Rapporteur Mr. Doudou Diène attested to this remarkable state of mind when he noted

> . . . that, despite everything, this polarization, in all communities and at all levels of society, has resulted not in feelings of hatred between communities but rather in a culture of fear and mistrust which pervades all social activity. During his meetings and interviews, he also noted the existence of a sense of belonging at all levels of society. Therefore, at the basic level of the people's deepest feelings, Guyanese society does nurture the human values necessary for overcoming ethnic polarization and collectively building genuine pluralism, through which a dynamic, creative balance could enable cultural and spiritual differences to be recognized, respected, protected and promoted and universal values arising out of cross-fertilization among communities to be cultivated. . . . The story of Guyana is, to a deeply disturbing degree, the story of political exploitation of the race factor . . . .

The new political operatives push a racist and other biased line to sustain a culture of fear and mistrust among the people of this country. This negative culture is presented to the people. But the people at large have not created this negativism. The negative culture of race hate is not part of the Guyanese people's personality. However, the Guyanese people must know the source(s) of this fear and mistrust. The source is the political-mass media-racial complex that together has wrought havoc on the Guyanese people and the nation-building program. We need to keep in mind that sometimes we hear the loudest yelps for freedom from the drivers of race hate.

Where is Racial Domination in Guyana?

A Book Review of 'The Cycle of Racial Oppression in Guyana' by Kean Gibson

The Ethnic Relations Commission (ERC) has now ruled on allegations of racism against Kean Gibson's book, 'The Cycle of Racial Oppression in Guyana'. The ERC's ruling in part noted: "The Commission stresses that the author of the publication has advanced no facts whatsoever for the contention advanced that there exists an organized, systematic plan of oppression by Hindus/Indo-Guyanese of the Afro-Guyanese citizens of this country. Nor, in the public hearings undertaken by the Commission, was any evidence advanced to this effect, and the Commission is not otherwise aware of any evidence which would so suggest. The Commission emphasizes that the absence of such evidence in foundation of the thesis maintained by the author reduces the arguments advanced to mere hypothesis, supposition and opinion, unsubstantiated in fact and reality" (ERC Report, February 9, 2005).

In light of this development, here is a review of the Gibson book that I presented prior to the inquiry.

The motivation for domination is not whether a racial group is seen as good or evil, but whether the racial group has something that the power-holding group wants. The need to dominate may have a lot more to do with exploiting any means to achieve profit maximization. A class analysis, therefore, dissipates the potency of Gibson's dualism of good and evil in justifying domination.

Racial oppression conjures up images of African Americans in the Deep South prior to the ending of segregation in education through the U.S. Supreme Court's decision in the Brown v. Board of Education 1954 case, Africans in South Africa during Apartheid, Africans in Ian Smith's Rhodesia (now Zimbabwe), the genocide in Rwanda, genocide against Native American Indians, and Hitler's assault on Jews, among others. Some significant forms of racial domination are genocide, involuntary population transfer, forced assimilation, internal colonialism, and forced segregation. Do these forms of racial domination really describe Guyana? I think not.

The oppressed rapidly experience a sustained social and economic disadvantage and stigma, following their dispossession of all meaningful resources. The rewards of society, driving social status upwardly, are denied to the oppressed, producing a low socioeconomic status (SES) for them.

The SES is a measure of a person's combined score on education, occupational status, and income. The score determines a person's class position and assumes a continuum of inequality between classes. SES is directly correlated with class. Clearly, then, East Indians and Africans can be high on education, occupational status, and income, and indeed, some can be moderate, low, or even zero on these, as well.

A social class is a group of people who holds a similar position in the economic system of production, distribution, and consumption of goods and services in society. Most societies have a class structure for the entire society and another class structure for each ethnic group.

A recent book "The Cycle of Racial Oppression in Guyana" by Kean Gibson claims that East Indians oppress Africans in Guyana through the Hindu caste system oppression, she noted, is motivated through East Indians' desire to secure and sustain power. A justification for oppression, according to Gibson, is the use of the dualism of good and evil where Hindus see themselves as good, and perceive Africans as evil because of their black skin color. In fact, Gibson believes that the People's Progressive Party/Civic (PPP/C) has an agenda to create a racial state based on racial criteria, which could result in the extermination of Africans in the same way that Hitler attempted to eliminate Jews in Germany. What are we to make of these sweeping statements? Let's review the book.

The Caste System

Gibson's book indicts Hinduism as legitimizing racism through the caste system. The term 'caste' was an English derivation from the Portuguese word 'casta', used by the Portuguese to explain India's social structure, according to Malhotra. He said that the word 'caste' is not found in Sanskrit or any Indian language. One of the allusions to such a social structure is found in the Gita, chapter 4, verse 13 where the concept of 'varna' is elucidated. Chapter 4, verse 13 says, "The fourfold order was created by me according to the divisions of quality and work."

Varna initially was mistranslated as 'caste', which subsequently became institutionalized as the explanation of India's social structure. Later, the British census of India utilized rigid caste boundaries that classified the population. Total communities were categorized into a single occupational category which created a contrived Indian identity. Malhotra further noted, "Later, India's own government continued this caste division as a way to promote affirmative action, thereby exacerbating such divisive identities. Politicians found in the caste categories, what has been called 'vote banks' and this method of harvesting votes has caused social problems. Unfortunately, all this has been blamed on Hinduism by western scholars and their Indian followers."

Gibson erroneously sees Hinduism as the culprit in East Indian domination of Africans through the Hindu caste system. And Gibson presents caste as a mandatory requirement of Hinduism. This is a false interpretation. Dr. Sarvepalli Radhakrishnan, a former President of India, explains chapter 4, verse 13 of the Gita as "*caturvarnyam*: the fourfold order. The emphasis is on guna (aptitude) and karma (function) and not jati (birth). The varna or the order to which we belong is independent of sex, birth or breeding. A class determined by temperament and vocation is not a caste determined by birth and heredity. According to the Mahabharata, the whole world was originally of one class but later it became divided into four divisions on account of the specific duties. Even the distinction between caste and outcaste is artificial and unspiritual. An ancient verse points out that the Brahmin and the outcastes are blood brothers... . The fourfold order is designed for human evolution. There is nothing absolute about the caste system, which has changed its character in the process of history. Today it cannot be regarded as anything more than an insistence on a variety of ways in which the social purpose can be carried out. Functional groupings will never be out of date. . . . The present morbid condition of India broken into castes and sub-castes is opposed to the unity taught by the *Gita*, which stands for an organic as against an atomistic conception of society."

Swami Chinmayananda's explanation of this chapter 4, verse 13 of the Gita says "This is a stanza that has been much misused in recent times by the upholders of the social crime styled as the caste system in India. *Varna*, meaning different shades of texture, or colour, is employed here in the *Yogic*-sense. In the *Yoga Sastra*, they attribute some definite colours to the triple *gunas*, which mean, as we have said earlier, "the mental temperaments". Thus, *Sattwa* is considered as white, *Rajas* as red, and *Tamas* as black. Man is essentially the thoughts that he entertains. From individual to individual, even when the thoughts are superficially the same, there are clear distinctions recognizable from their temperaments."

"On the basis of these temperamental distinctions, the entire mankind has been, for the purpose of spiritual study, classified into four "castes" or *Varnas*. Just as, in a metropolis, on the basis of trade or professions, we divide the people as doctors, advocates, professors, traders, politicians, tongawalas, etc., so too, on the basis of the different textures of thoughts entertained by the intelligent creatures, the four "castes" had been labelled in the past. From the standpoint of the State, a doctor and a tongawala are as much important as an advocate and a mechanic. So too, for the perfectly healthy life of a society, all "castes" should not be competitive but cooperative units, each being complementary to the others, never competing among themselves."

I intentionally provide these long but significant quotes as interpretations of the varnas in chapter 4, verse 13 of the Gita because the essence of Gibson's book is that Hinduism through the caste system, legitimizes racial domination of Africans. Clearly, Dr. Radhakrishnan and Swami Chinmayananda's explanations of the caste system as applied in Hinduism cannot and will not support the view, that Hindus perceive Africans as evil because they are from the lowest caste. The lowest caste can move to the highest caste and each caste is not competing against one another, but infuses cooperative elements among each other. Indeed, Gibson fails to present the philosophical implications of the varnas in expounding the societal division of labor in Hindu theology.

At any rate, the Hindu caste system has nothing to do with skin color. Caste pertains to the qualities and actions of people. In Ancient India, these caste divisions were not based on birth, but on qualifications. Today, after three thousand years and the disintegration of the Aryan family structure, the caste system has deteriorated in India. The caste system in this degenerative form has little or no relevance or application to Guyana today, even among the Hindus themselves. Keep in mind that the Gita did not reference the word 'caste'; the Gita uses the word 'varnas'.

Dualism of Good & Evil

Gibson's use of dualism, on its own, as a theoretical framework, to provide explanations of racial oppression is inadequate. Why? This pernicious dualism of good and evil is seen as two separate extreme options. These options are not allowed to draw from each other because they are seen as two separate sides. The reality, however, is that those East Indians who see themselves as good also may see other East Indians and other ethnics as evil, and which may have nothing to do with the caste system. Both East Indians and Africans seen as evil, theoretically, can occupy any caste position. The lowest caste is not the only bearer of evil, contrary to what Gibson enunciates; other castes also are carriers of evil. Further, there may be cases where Africans perceived as evil do not experience exploitation, contradicting Gibson's main argument. Why? Africans seen as evil also may wield power that would prevent any domination perpetrated on them by anyone or group. If these Africans are perceived as evil and have the capacity to dominate others, then to what caste do they belong? These Africans, therefore, cannot belong to the lowest caste, as Gibson suggests, for the lowest caste will not have the capacity to dominate.

Only those East Indians and Africans in positions of power will have the capacity to exploit those East Indians and Africans without power. Further, these East Indians and Africans without power may both be perceived simultaneously as having characteristics of both good and evil. But the caste system and evil are not the sole determinants of power in any society. This capacity to dominate is determined by a person's class position in society, that is, whether the person is located in the upper, middle or lower classes. Evidently, then, occupancy of a caste and an 'evil' typecast are not sufficient preconditions to dominate another group. This argument seriously undermines Gibson's use of caste as an explanation of domination against Africans.

Do all East Indians also exploit all Africans categorized as evil? Keep in mind working, lower, and under classes of any racial group, by definition, will not have the power to dominate any other group. If any East Indian oppression of Africans occurs, then it will have to emanate from those East Indians in the higher social classes. Using this line of argument, only lower class Africans and not upper class Africans may experience domination. The lower classes of any group will have limited resources to resist exploitation or even to direct oppression at any group or individual. Indeed, this perspective demonstrates that Africans with appropriate resources also could dominate other ethnic groups. Clearly, the group's capacity is a stronger precondition to dominate than caste and 'evil' projection, further deflating the explanatory value of Gibson's cycle of racial oppression.

Do upper-class East Indians see their African upper-class counterparts as evil? Research findings suggest that classes at the same level, even from different racial and ethnic groups, tend to support and effect greater interaction with each other. Therefore, people with resources from different racial groups, may attempt to dominate others from different racial groups who have little or no resources and also are perceived as having characteristics of both good and evil. The motivation for domination is not whether a racial group is seen as good or evil, but whether the racial group has something that the power-holding group wants. The need to dominate may have a lot more to do with exploiting any means to achieve profit maximization. A class analysis, therefore, dissipates the potency of Gibson's dualism of good and evil in justifying domination.

Good and evil in dualism are presented in terms of either one option or another and the 'good' option is generally presented as the proper option, as exemplified in Gibson's work. But options presented as competing alternatives are not necessarily in opposition because good and evil are recursive in social life, and together they constantly adjust to each other in accordance with the social class dynamics of behavioral demands. Therefore, good and evil, simultaneously, can be found in any group and be integral to that group's behavior. Undoubtedly, Gibson's quest to make East Indians the paragon of evil in a multiethnic society ignores the simultaneous presence of good and evil in group behavior, a simultaneity well accepted today as a cultural universal in all ethnic groups.

Further, we have established that Guyana has upper and middle-class Africans who are unlikely to be victims of East Indian domination. Indeed, these Africans through their high socioeconomic status, cannot belong to Gibson's Sudra caste (lowest caste), as this caste, by definition, only will comprise people with low to zero socioeconomic status. Caste as a type of closed structured inequality, as presented by Gibson, is relatively fixed, and allows no social mobility. Clearly, upper and middle-class Africans in Guyana are upwardly mobile and, therefore, are a manifest contradiction to any 'low caste' placement of Africans, as used by Gibson. East Indians, too, who lack resources, can be victims of domination, and those East Indians with resources, will experience upward social mobility.

The SES of East Indians & Africans

The book noted, among other things, that the PPP/C Government is in the throes of creating an African underclass using racial criteria. The concept of underclass may refer to people who are poor and chronically unemployed. People from the underclass experience a sustained social and economic disadvantage and stigma, following their dispossession of all meaningful resources. In effect, the underclass will have a low socio-economic status (SES). Let's offer just a few examples to show how Africans are doing, in order to debunk this mistaken claim.

Social marginalization of Africans means that Africans do not participate fully in the occupational structures in Guyana. This is not true, as evidenced from my publication on *Social Marginalization, A Preliminary Study*. Let us review some evidence from this study and use just a few examples. Africans have substantial levels of participation at the University of Guyana, in the public service, especially among senior administrative and executive positions, the State Boards in Education and comparably represented on other State Boards. In 1989, the public service minimum wage was $595 (US$59.50). Today, the public service minimum wage is in excess of $20,045 (US$105).

Region 4, with a large African population, obtained $148 million budgetary allocation in 2001, and this allocation does not include Georgetown with a substantial African population. The Regional Administration of Region 4, apportioned $85.7 million to mainly African areas which include BV, Ann's Grove, Bagotstown, Melanie Damishana, Paradise, Bladen Hall, Victoria, Golden Grove, Plaisance, Buxton, Vryheid's Lust, and Nabaclis. The budgetary allocations are higher for this Fiscal Year. People who are marginalized and dominated do not receive sizable budgetary allocations.

The major ethnic groups in Guyana are well represented among the SSEE (Secondary Schools Entrance Examination) passes as well as among the CXC Examination successes. In this year's SSEE results, 40 out of the top 104 candidates are Africans. Generally, the SES for both Africans and East Indians is relatively comparable. A review of groups' education, occupational status, and income will demonstrate their spectacular achievements and successes.

In 2000, students with 5 or more Grade Ones at the CXC were from mixed schools with large proportions of Africans and East Indians. These were President's College, Berbice High, Anna Regina Multilateral, New Amsterdam Multilateral, Bishop's High, St. Joseph's High, Brickdam Secondary, and Queen's College. Africans compared to East Indians have relatively higher job status in the Public Service, among positions as Permanent Secretary, Deputy Permanent Secretary, Principal Assistant Secretary, Assistant Secretary, Accountant Head, and Senior Personnel Officer. Most school heads are Africans in the Nursery, Primary, and Secondary Schools. Five out of the 10 Regional Education Officers are Africans. Africans are in a majority on the State Boards in Education. At the University of Guyana, Africans constitute a majority of faculty members. Africans predominate in the disciplined forces. Data indicates that Africans receive 70% and East Indians and others 30% of house lots. Equitable budgetary provisions are allocated for African and East Indian neighborhoods.

The evidence does not support Gibson's argument that East Indians dominate Africans or even that Africans are victims of domination perpetrated by other people.

Just as social marginalization of Africans is fictional, likewise political marginalization is unreal. I want now merely to reiterate what I said in previous commentaries on the question of the inclusiveness of the existing political system. Joint committees as one component emerging out of the Dialog achieved substantial gains. With a continuance of the Dialog now called Constructive Engagement, greater gains can evolve. It's an evolving process. The Constitutional Commissions represent another component making for inclusiveness, and these are the Ethnic Relations Commission, Women and Gender Equality Commission, Indigenous People's Commission, Commission for the Rights of the Child, and the Human Rights Commission. In addition, there are the Sectoral Committees in Parliament and the Parliamentary Management Committee. All of these measures—Dialog, Constructive Engagement, including joint committees, commissions, and parliamentary committees—can substantially contribute to developing institutionalized structures of inclusiveness of all ethnic groups. And of course, the role of a responsible opposition is a trump card still waiting to be played. Where is this racial domination of Africans by East Indians?

Unconvincing Sources

Gibson's book is punctuated with numerous unauthentic sources. Referencing Sidney King's (now Eusi Kwayana) booklet "Next Witness", Gibson describes the vulgarities perpetrated against Africans by East Indians during the 1961 PPP victory motorcade. Gibson then makes the quantum leap, suggesting that these emotional expressions against Africans pertain to the Hindu definition

and treatment of the lowest caste. Surely, many East Indians in the victory
march were not all Hindus, as participants would also have included East Indian
Muslims and East Indian Christians. Muslims and Christians do not accept the
caste system goes another Gibson goof!!

The composition of State Boards is based on racial criteria, another claim
that should have been verified. Africans dominate the State Boards in Education.
In a review of 27 other State Boards, Africans are in a majority on 13, East Indians in a majority on 12, and two have equal numbers from these two ethnic
groups. Gibson goofs again!!

The Guyana Defense Force (GDF) is not in a state of preparedness because
the current Government has made no inadequate budgetary allocation since
1992, another erroneous Gibson remark. The table below shows the true story.

Table 2.3: Guyana Defense Force Expenditure 1990-2003

Year	G.D.F	
	Current (Gm$000)	**Capital (Gm$000)**
1990	185.2	0.3
1991	322.4	0.7
1992	599.3	7
1993	709.4	11
1994	973	50.5
1995	1,457.80	79.9
1996	1,246.80	88.3
1997	1,325.90	69.2
1998	1,378.40	90.7
1999	1,538.00	112.4
2000	1,954.30	472
2001	2,291.147	42
2002	2,624.857	42
2003	2,737.68	43
TOTAL	19,344.186	1109

Source: GINA

Today, the GDF's current expenditure is almost $3 billion and the capital ex-
penditure is $43 million compared to measly pre-1993 budgetary allocations.
The GDF has had a consistent increase in budgetary allocations in the PPP/C
years.

It's far from the truth to suggest that the PPP/C Government destroyed the
Guyana National Service (GNS), again another inaccurate Gibson remark. Several GNS Centers were set up in the early 1970s and 1980s.But early closures
started in 1984 and declining enrolment commenced just after 1980. Limited

enrolment and financial problems accounted for the closures. It was the People's National Congress (PNC) Party in Government at the time, not the PPP.

These are some of the many examples of allegations and sources not authenticated, as is normally required in serious academic research. We, therefore, can only surmise that the book is a symbolism of racial acrimony and provides a spurious explanation for any racism prevailing in this country.

References

Andersen, Margaret L. and Patricia Hill Collins, eds. 1992. *Race, Class and Gender*. Belmont, CA: Wadsworth.

Appadurai, A.1996.Modernity at Large: Cultural Dimensions of Globalization. Minneapolis, MN: University of Minnesota Press.

Balasubramanyam, V.N. and Wei, Y. 2006. "Diaspora and Development", In *The World Economy:* Volume 29 Issue. University of Lancaster.

Berry, Brewton and Henry L. Tischler.1978.*Race and Ethnic Relations.*4th ed. Boston, MA: Houghton Mifflin Company.

Boodhoo, Martin J. and Baksh, Ahamad. 1981. *The Impact of Brain Drain on Development: A Case Study of Guyana*. ESCOR, ODA, Government of U.K. & the University of Manchester, University of Guyana

Cross, Malcolm.1980.*The East Indians of Guyana and Trinidad*. 2nd. ed. London, England: Minority Rights Group.

Debiprasad, Sahadeo and Dowlat, Ram Budhram. 1987. "East Indians in the Caribbean." In *Indians in the Caribbean*, ed. I.J. Bahadur Singh. New Delhi, India: Sterling Publishers Private Limited.

Gibson, Kean. 2004. The Cycle of Racial Oppression in Guyana. Lanham, MD: The University Press of America.

Gordon, M.M.1964.*Assimilation in American Life*. New York: Oxford University Press.

Greene, Felix. 1971. *The Enemy: What Every American Should Know about Imperialism*. New York: Vintage Books.

Hildyard, Nicholas.1999. *"Blood" and "Culture" - Ethnic Conflict and the Authoritarian Right.* CornerHouse Briefing 11.Dorset, England: CornerHouse.

Jagan, Cheddi. 1997. The West on Trial: My Fight for Guyana's Freedom. St. John's, Antigua: Hansib Caribbean

Jayawardena, Chandra. 1963. *Conflict and Solidarity on a Guianese Plantation*. London: Berg Publisher of Oxford International Publishers Ltd.

Klass, Morton. 1961. *East Indians in Trinidad: A Study of Cultural Persistence*. New York: Columbia University Press.

Medler, Jerry and Medler, Michael. 1996. Media Images as Environmental Policy. In *Society and the Media: A Collection of Essays,* ed. Marilyn J. Carter. New York: HarperCollins Publishers.

Misir, Prem. Forthcoming. *Ethnic Cleavage & Closure in the Caribbean Diaspora: Essays on Race, Ethnicity, & Class.* Lewiston, New York: Edwin Mellen Press.

Naipaul, V.S.1975. "A Plea for Rationality," Address *to the Conference on East Indians in the Caribbean – Beyond Survival,* University of the West Indies, St. Augustine, Trinidad & Tobago.

Nath, Dwarka. 1970. *A History of Indians in British Guiana,* 2nd revised ed. London: Thomas Nelson & Sons.

Newman, William M.1973.*American Pluralism: A Study of Minority Groups and Social Theory.* New York: Harper and Row.

Ocampo, Jose Antonio. 2006. World Economic Situation and Prospects.

Ortega Y Gasset, Jose.Mildred Adams (Translator).1996.*Invertebrate Spain.* Library Binding, Fertig Howard Inc.

Rodney, Walter.1982.*A History of the Guyanese Working People, 1881-1905.*Baltimore, MD: The Johns Hopkins University Press.

Shively, W. Phillips.1997.*Power and Choice: An Introduction to Political Science.*5th ed. New York: McGraw-Hill.

Smith, M.G.1965.*The Plural Society in the British West Indies.* Berkeley, CA: University of California Press.

Tinker, Hugh. 1974. *A New System of Slavery: The Export of Indian Labor Overseas, 1830-1920,* Oxford University Press.

Truman, Harry. Speech at Baylor University, March 6, 1947.

World Bank Report 1994.

World Bank. The Global Economic Prospect, 2006.

Index

About the Editor

Prem Misir is Pro-Chancellor, University of Guyana; he was Executive Director of the Government Information Agency, Permanent Secretary of the Ministry of Information, Government of Guyana, and Chairman of the Guyana Broadcasting Corporation. Dr. Misir has been a Clinical Associate Professor, New York University, Faculty member, Baruch College/City University of New York, Assistant Professor at St. John's University, and Metropolitan College of New York. He was the Associate Public Health Epidemiologist at the Bureau of HIV Program Services, New York City Department of Health. Dr. Misir was Research & Evaluation Coordinator—Graduate Medical Education, United Hospitals Medical Center/UMDNJ, and Assistant Professor & Primary Care Coordinator, Interfaith Medical Center/SUNYHSCB. He was also a Research Fellow and a Lecturer at the University of Guyana. Prem Misir received his Ph.D. from the University of Hull, England, the M.Phil (Master of Philosophy) from the University of Surrey, England, the B.S.Sc. (Honors) from the Queen's University of Belfast, U.K. Dr. Misir is also the author of several books, including *Leader Behavior and the Compliance Structure In Education: A Sociological Study of Ideology and Social Change in Guyana* (Medgar Evers College/CUNY, Caribbean Diaspora Press, 1998), *Workers' Participation in Management* (New Delhi, India: Reliance Publishing House, 1995), *Work Commitment in Education: An International Perspective* (New Delhi, India: Reliance Publishing House, 1995). He co-edited *The East Indian Diaspora* (New York: Asian American Center, Queens College/CUNY, 1993); his articles have appeared in several journals, including *AIDS Patient Care and STDs, Journal of Indo Caribbean Research, and TransAfrica Forum*. Dr. Misir is currently completing a book manuscript on *Marginalization in Guyana*.